Dear Husband [...]

my hard [...]

Ann I have [...]

Both times of her

confindolments and

by the gating on

gain

ve hall sends our

neurst and dearted

Love to you

with a 1000 kiss

Dear Husband you

must excuse writing

These Few Lines

These Few Lines

A CONVICT STORY

THE LOST LIVES OF MYRA & WILLIAM SYKES

GRAHAM SEAL

ABC
Books

Published by ABC Books for the
AUSTRALIAN BROADCASTING CORPORATION
GPO Box 9994 Sydney NSW 2001

First published in 2006

National Library of Australia
Cataloguing-in-Publication Entry
Seal, Graham, 1950– .
These few lines : a convict story : the lost lives of Myra
& William Sykes.

Bibliography.
ISBN 10: 0 7333 1948 3
ISBN 13: 978 0 7333 1948 8

1. Sykes, William, 1827-1891. 2. Sykes, Myra.
3. Convicts – Western Australia – Biography.
4. Prisoners' spouses – England – Sheffield – Biography.
5. Convicts – Western Australia – Correspondence. I. Title.

994.102092

Cover and internal design by Christabella Designs
Typeset in 10.5 on 14pt Sabon by Kirby Jones
Colour reproduction by Graphic Print Group, Adelaide
Printed by Quality Printing, Hong Kong, China

5 4 3 2 1

CONTENTS

INTRODUCTION

Obscure Ghosts

It was a freezing December day when I walked on the green Yorkshire field that is now St Mary's churchyard, Greasbrough. I had come to meet a woman, dead for over a century. But the last resting place of Myra Sykes could not be found. Together with all the other headstones that once filled this churchyard, Myra's had long gone.

The echoes of the final hymn faded into the grey stone walls as the minister farewelled the small congregation at the door. In response to my inquiry about the unusual absence of weathered memorials to the dead in an English churchyard, the robed clergyman said that there had been no graves in the churchyard for a good many years and he was uncertain about what might have happened to all the old headstones. He thought they might be found in the municipal cemetery a few miles up the road.

Some weeks earlier I had walked through the dry heat of a cemetery in rural Western Australia looking for the grave of Myra's transported husband, William. The cemetery was dotted with the crosses, urns and other memorials to pioneers, farmers and workers usually seen in bush graveyards. But William Sykes's last resting place in the sand of Western Australia's matter-of-fact Toodyay cemetery was also nowhere to be found.

I was searching the far ends of the earth for the last remains of two obscure ghosts whose story of love, hardship and endurance had survived by chance in a few of Myra's scribbled letters, William's brief shipboard journal and later letters to his brothers and sister, together with one written by his son; there was also a handful of official documents. Time and change had obliterated almost all other physical traces of these two human beings. Without these few tattered remnants of a long-forgotten relationship, a tale spanning decades, hemispheres and hearts would have been entirely buried in the past.

The bare bones of this story are that William Sykes, husband to Myra and father of their four children, was transported for life to Western Australia in 1867. He had been convicted of killing a gamekeeper during a poaching affray in Silver Wood, near Rotherham in England's South Yorkshire. The diary he kept during the voyage to Australia, together with the letters Myra and his children sent to him over 24 years of separation are a moving record of a woman's courage, determination and unflinching love for her family, against all the odds.

These documents, held in a roughly-made kangaroo-skin pouch, were discovered in 1931 during the demolition of the old police buildings at Toodyay, a colonial town about 100 kilometres north-east of Perth, Western Australia. The pouch and its contents came into the hands of a member of the Western Australian Historical Society. Some members of the Society's Council believed the letters had little historical worth and so should be destroyed. Fortunately, the honorary secretary of the Society, Paul Hasluck, later to have a distinguished career in Australian public life and scholarship, convinced his colleagues to preserve the letters, made a copy of them and generally interested himself in their fate, as did his wife, Alexandra Hasluck.

In 1934 the matter of the letters again came before the Western Australian Historical Society in a fiery meeting during which different views were forcefully expressed about whether to keep or destroy the scraps of paper. The issues at stake were various. One strong faction held that the letters were personal and therefore not historical documents. Another felt they were related to the convict era of Western Australian history, a period that many at that time wished only to forget. Some thought the preservation of the letters constituted a trust that it was their responsibility to honour for posterity.

The preservers won the day and the kangaroo-skin pouch was left with the Society for safekeeping. So safely were the letters kept, says Alexandra Hasluck in the prologue to her book *Unwilling Emigrants* in which these details are recounted, 'that nothing more was heard of them, no research done on them'. Almost two decades later, Alexandra Hasluck came across her husband's copies of the letters and wondered if the originals were still in existence. She found them in what was then the Archives Department of the State Library of Western Australia. Two envelopes had disappeared, along with the kangaroo-skin pouch, and another letter had appeared from an unknown source. Alexandra Hasluck embarked on extensive research in Australia and in England to find out all she could about Myra and William Sykes. The results of this work are included in her classic study of the convict period in Western Australia, first published in 1959 and reprinted a number of times since, most recently in 2002.

I first came across the compelling story of Myra and William Sykes when moving to Western Australia in the mid-1980s. I wanted to find out something about the place and, one lunchtime, while I was browsing in the bins of the many remainder bookshops that then dotted Sydney, I came across *Unwilling Emigrants*. In this brief but passionately researched and written history of transportation to the Swan River colony I read for the first time the letters of Myra, some of her children's and the shipboard jottings of William Sykes.

The fragmentary letters hinted at a tale of two ordinary people flung together by the ravages of the Industrial Revolution, then torn apart by the grinding of a remorseless legal machine. It was a story of a time, of two places and of a number of human beings enmeshed in processes not only beyond their control, but also largely beyond their knowing. It was also, as I was to discover, a story that held many mysteries and more than a few surprises.

When I reached Perth I searched out the documents in the Battye Library of Western Australia. Still fascinated by what I then knew of the tale, I based a radio feature on them for the Australian Broadcasting Commission, as it was then called. Some years later, still drawn by the poignancy of the Sykes saga, I wrote an article about it for the British historical magazine, *History Today*. It seemed then that this was enough and Myra, William and their children were best left in peace.

But then my work took me back to that part of England where Myra and William had spent their childhoods and their early married lives, and where Myra lived until her death. When I first visited Sheffield, Rotherham and surrounding areas many of the houses, streets, villages and suburbs that Myra and William called home were still there, much as they had been all those years ago. Slowly, the story of these sundered lives found its way back into my own life. I gradually realised that the only way to lay these obscure but compelling ghosts to rest was to write this book.

Beginning to work seriously at this task I discovered that it was not to be as straightforward as I had supposed. I began with the known, if limited, historical sources. The letters, lists and brief diary were still held by the Battye Library of Western Australian History. They provided a starting point for other documentation about William Sykes's sojourn within the penal bureaucracy of the Swan River colony. These records fleshed out the basic details of this part of the story, though there was little about Myra Sykes and the family beyond the contents of her letters.

Other leads uncovered a number of new documents not known to previous researchers. These included the accounts of the surgeon and religious instructor aboard the ship that transported William to the Swan River. Even more excitingly, another letter, written by the local vicar on behalf of one of William and Myra's grown-up sons had found its way into the archives. Penned in 1891, the letter petitioned for the release and repatriation of William Sykes, after nearly 30 years of servitude and separation from family and friends. The sad ironies of this letter are detailed in the following pages.

Later still, the few available clues presented a number of new mysteries. Among these were the whereabouts of William Sykes's last resting place, the possibility that the family had made an earlier attempt to have him repatriated and that the documentary evidence for this was contained in the archives – somewhere. There was even the odd wrinkle that a French academic had made extensive enquiries into the Sykes story during the early 1990s, though nothing further seems to have been heard of this interest. Most intriguing of all was the possibility that some, at least, of the descendants of William and Myra Sykes had been tracked down. The further I delved into these matters, long past and relatively recent, the more intriguing the story became.

Further research into the Sykes genealogy and the local history of Rotherham revealed a number of surprises. In the archives I found two previously unknown letters from William Sykes, writing back to his family in England. Another surprise revealed yet one more very important unknown detail of this very human story.

Alexandra Hasluck's book concentrated mainly on the fate of William Sykes, cast away at the far end of the planet. She evoked the transportation system and the state of the Swan River colony's administrative and legal machinery. My book is about the relationship of Myra and William as revealed, necessarily in fragmentary form, through their surviving correspondence and the surviving records. It also restores the balance of the story by discovering much more about the circumstances leading up to William Sykes's conviction for manslaughter and revealing what happened to Myra and the children during and after the long years of William's exile.

Researching and writing this book has been something like a historical detective mystery, with various clues leading to the gradual filling in of most of the jigsaw. The jigsaw remains incomplete, as all historical resurrections must. Yet it doesn't matter. Myra and William's story goes beyond history. What is really enduring about it is their relationship, difficult though that was, especially for Myra. The details of economic, social and political forces beyond the control of individuals and of the oppressions wrought by various legal and penal machineries are fleeting. What persists and what speaks to most of us today is the human dimension of the distant past and a constant wife's loyalty to her dear husband.

AUTHOR'S NOTE

A NOTE ON THE SPELLING
Place names, and almost everything else, were spelled variously in the nineteenth century, even within the same document. Greasbrough was also Greasebrough, Gresbro and Greasbro similarly for Masbrough, Masbro, etc. For consistency, I have used the most common English renditions, Greasbrough and Masborough. Spellings in primary source documents are as they originally appeared.

Even more variable is the spelling in letters and other documents penned – or perhaps sometimes dictated – by Myra, William and others. Despite the occasional difficulty in translating some of the words, I have preferred to leave these as in the originals. Where necessary, an occasional clarification is provided in square brackets.

Full transcriptions of the letters and selected other documents are provided in the Appendix, again in the original spelling.

A NOTE ON THE USE OF IMPERIAL MEASUREMENTS
While it is conventional publishing practice to change imperial measurements to metric measure, or to parenthetically insert a metric conversion immediately after the imperial, I felt it was more appropriate and authentic to retain only the original measurements.

These Few Lines

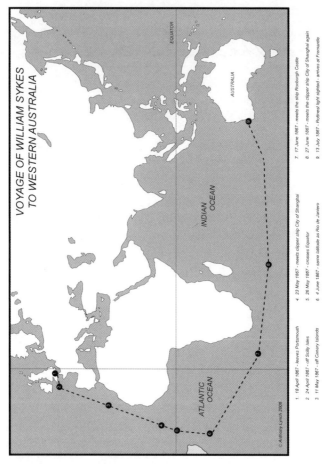

VOYAGE OF WILLIAM SYKES
TO WESTERN AUSTRALIA

EQUATOR

AUSTRALIA

INDIAN
OCEAN

ATLANTIC
OCEAN

© Anthony Lynch 2005

1. 18 April 1867 - leaves Portsmouth

2. 24 April 1867 - off Scilly Isles

3. 11 May 1867 - off Canary Islands

4. 23 May 1867 - meets clipper ship City of Shanghai

5. 26 May 1867 - crosses Equator

6. 4 June 1867 - same latitude as Rio de Janeiro

7. 17 June 1867 - meets the ship Roxburgh Castle

8. 27 June 1867 - meets the clipper ship City of Shanghai again

9. 13 July 1867 - Rottnest light sighted - arrives at Fremantle

The voyage of the Norwood from Portsmouth to the Swan River,
April–June, 1867. (Map by Anthony Lynch)

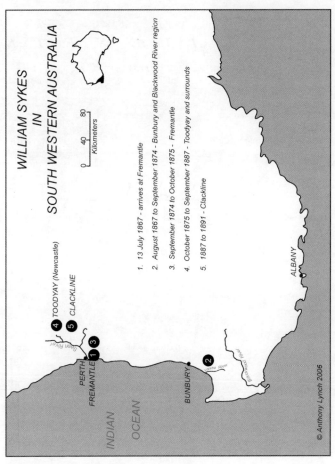

WILLIAM SYKES
IN
SOUTH WESTERN AUSTRALIA

0   40   80
Kilometers

1. 13 July 1867 - arrives at Fremantle

2. August 1867 to September 1874 - Bunbury and Blackwood River region

3. September 1874 to October 1875 - Fremantle

4. October 1875 to September 1887 - Toodyay and surrounds

5. 1887 to 1891 - Clackline

TOODYAY (Newcastle)

CLACKLINE

PERTH

FREMANTLE

Swan River

BUNBURY

Blackwood River

ALBANY

INDIAN

OCEAN

© Anthony Lynch 2006

South-West of the Swan River colony showing places where William Sykes lived, worked and died, 1867–1891. (Map by Anthony Lynch)

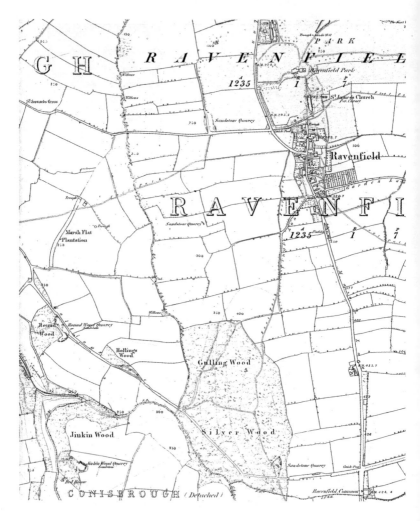

Silver Wood as it was in the Nineteenth Century. Surveyed 1850–1851, published 1854. Scale 1 mile to 6 inches. (Rotherham Metropolitan Borough Council, Archives and Local Studies)

1   *By Silver Wood*

> *Me and five more a-poaching went.*
> *To get some game was our intent,*
> *Our money being gone and spent,*
> *We'd nothing left to try.*
>
> 'Bill Brown', poaching ballad

Hanging over a valley of belching chimneys and fiery forges, Silver Wood was little more than remnant wilderness as the Industrial Revolution reached white heat in the 1860s. Before the creeping demands of steel and profit blighted the country around Rotherham much of the area had been lightly treed woodlands edged with open fields. In these forests and furrows generations of Yorkshiremen had pursued their ancient custom of poaching. Traditionally, game was taken to supplement diets and, in some cases, to augment incomes as the restaurants of the developing cities provided a ready, if illicit, market for hare, rabbit and pheasant. The owners of these resources were, of course, not happy about this plundering of their larders and took increasingly elaborate and brutal steps to secure their 'rights' against poaching. But the poachers were a hardy lot of stubborn Yorkshire types, undeterred by these attempts to contain their pleasures. The taking of a rabbit or two, perhaps a pheasant, was economically useful. It was good healthy sport as well, and it also provided an opportunity for thumbing noses at the upper classes, a custom as deeply ingrained in Yorkshire working-class life as poaching itself.

William Sykes and those who were to be his poaching companions one fatal night were Yorkshire working men. They were employed – on and off – in the urban and industrial enterprises of coal mining and metal smelting. But though the effects of industrialism were already profound, those who sweated aboveground or below were often born and bred in the countryside surrounding the rapidly expanding conurbations of Sheffield, Rotherham and Manchester. If not, rarely were they more than one generation removed from those who had been. The ways of the country were familiar to them and usually within easy access. As the cities, with their forges and factories, bloated outwards, so too did the working-class suburbs clustering at their fringes. Often, it was simply a matter of jumping over the back wall to be out into the surrounding fields and woods.

It was nothing much out of the ordinary for working men such as David Booth, Aaron 'Ginger' Savage, John Teale, Henry Bone, John Bentcliffe and Robert Woodhouse to meet at the house of Myra and William Sykes in the smoky village of Masborough, as they did around round six in the evening of 10 October 1865. Four of the men had been busy making rabbit nets for the game they planned to poach near Silver Wood, just a few miles away. But this night-poaching expedition was to have life-shattering consequences for every one of those in the Sykes house that Tuesday evening, especially the lives of William and Myra and those of their children.

William Sykes, like most working-class men and boys in this part of the world, worked in the steel and allied industries, having started at the coal pits at an early age. He was a puddler, employed at the dangerous task of stirring molten metal from the furnaces at the ironworks just across the road, though he had been unemployed for some months.[1] Since marrying Myra 12 years before, he had marginally improved his circumstances, spurred on by the need to feed four children. While William and Myra were not compelled to take lodgers into the house, there was rarely enough to make ends meet. Any chance of bagging something extra for the table, or perhaps to sell for some much-needed cash, was eagerly sought, especially if it provided an opportunity for a little outdoor recreation, the thrill of outsmarting the keepers and the chance for some rough male camaraderie.

The men who met at the Sykes house were William's usual companions, much of his own station and background, though their ages varied. Robert Woodhouse was 'a powerful-looking man' around 40 years old, with a chequered past as a publican and subcontractor. John Teale, at 36, was the tallest of the group, most of whom were under five feet six inches and solidly built in the traditional Yorkshire manner. Henry Bone, in his mid-thirties and an inveterate poacher from nearby Kimberworth, was accompanied by his lodger, John Bentcliffe, a ne'er-do-well in his early thirties. Aaron 'Ginger' Savage, 35 years old and known by a number of aliases, boarded at The Miner's Tavern in the village of New York. In his early 50s David Booth, who dressed like a fisherman, was the oldest of the gang. He lived precariously in the yard of the same pub where Savage boarded. Like most adult men of their background in this place, all were experienced poachers. Bentcliffe in particular was a notorious night walker, well known to local police.

Myra was at home seeing to the evening meal, doing household chores and getting the children settled down for the night. Busy though she was, she must have been worried about what her husband and his friends were up to. She knew they were going poaching because William was upstairs seeing to his nets. He came downstairs with them and after some further brief arrangements the men prepared to leave.

Dressed in velvet jackets and fustian trousers, carrying nets and armed with three-foot sticks, the seven poachers left the Sykes house through the back door. In two separate groups they carefully made their way through a coal yard along Clough Road. With Woodhouse, Bone and Bentcliffe in the lead, the poachers went down Gin House Lane to Carr House Colliery. Here they were seen by two men who would later be called as witnesses against them. As they proceeded they came across a man they thought may have been a policeman. Widely skirting him, they continued to Aldewarke pit.

By now it was dark, but a bright moon was rising, intermittently darkened by clouds.[2] This 'poacher's moon' made it an ideal night for trapping someone else's game. In case they met with any interference from the keepers of the Silver Wood game rights, the poachers filled their pockets with fist-sized glass cinders, leftovers of the furnaces. The men snared three rabbits in fields near Blacking Mill, then continued stealthily on towards their ultimate destination.

Silver Wood was owned by a local farmer who leased the shooting rights to retired Rotherham solicitor, Mr Henry Jubb – Justice of the Peace, Chairman of the Bench of Magistrates – and a syndicate of other gentlemen. Jubb hired keepers to protect his rights from the likes of William Sykes and his mates. The head keeper was a man called John Hawkins; he was assisted by Henry Machin and William Lilley. That night, for some reason, perhaps suspecting poaching activity, the keepers brought along another man to help them, a labourer named William Butler. The keepers were heavily armed. Lilley carried knuckle-dusters, a double-barrelled pistol and a 'teaser', a stick of wood about 20 inches in length with a heavy wooden ball on a flexible thong attached to one end, with the other end attached to his wrist by a loop of leather. The others were not so lethally equipped but still, they had come out into that crisp October night better prepared for trouble than the poachers.

All four keepers were well hidden in the bushes by 8 pm. About 10 o'clock they heard and saw three of Sykes's gang netting for rabbits in the field next to the wood. Muttering 'Now is our time', Lilley rose and led the keepers through the hedge. The poachers spotted them almost at once. One of them, probably Sykes, called out a warning to his mates: 'Hey up, lads, they're here.' As Lilley advanced towards the poachers, a tall man materialised from the darkness of the hedge and smashed a heavy stick down onto his skull. A hail of furnace cinders battered the heads of Machin and Butler. There was fighting and shouting; even the keepers' dogs were fighting the poachers' dogs. The cursing and barking brought the other four poachers running to the aid of their companions and a short but brutal struggle followed.

After a clout on the skull with a cinder furnace or rock the head keeper Hawkins went, he claimed, for help, but not before he saw what Butler also witnessed. Butler had been knocked down twice, remaining on the ground the second time. From this position he saw three of the poachers crashing their sticks down again and again on the unconscious body of Lilley. Dragging himself upright, Butler was making an unsteady escape when the poachers chased after him and beat him to the ground again. Fearing the same fate as Lilley he begged for mercy from William Sykes who was hitting him relentlessly. 'Don't pay me any more, and I'll never come again', he cried in terror and pain. Just then Woodhouse returned from chasing Machin and caught hold of Sykes, yelling, 'For God's sake, don't kill the man. Come away.' Sykes dropped his shattered stick, allowing Butler to rise and lurch off into the darkness. Woodhouse and Sykes returned to where Lilley lay. Woodhouse thwacked Lilley's leg to see if the keeper was alive. Lilley did not move.

This short, savage incident took perhaps five minutes. It eerily echoed the plots of many poaching songs and tales, with the poachers being surprised by well-armed keepers, a vicious, swearing scuffle of desperate men and dogs ending in the death of a poacher or a keeper, followed by the inevitable retribution of the law. In this real-life story it was keeper Lilley who would die of his wounds. He suffered because of the closeness of the community to which both the poachers and the keepers belonged. Sykes and Teale knew Lilley and he knew them. And they knew he could identify them if they did not knock him out before he recognised them.

But Sykes had panicked. Even though it was Teale who struck the blow that first brought Lilley down, Sykes seemingly finished the job. The poachers had then grabbed up their nets, separated the still-snarling dogs and nervously discussed their next move. They thought the police would be upon them before they had time to return home. So rather than go back through the same byways that had brought them, the wily Woodhouse took the gang along an alternative route, leaving the scene of the fracas far behind.

About an hour after the poachers fled, head keeper Hawkins returned with reinforcements. They found Lilley huddled on the frozen ground. According to the various published accounts, Lilley was gravely damaged with multiple skull fractures and eight wounds. They managed to carry him home but he suffered a brain haemorrhage and died the next day.

Although the events in Silver Wood were bloodily sensational, they were only the latest in a long tradition of British poaching that was an amalgam of social protest and economic need, stretching back to the mediaeval era.[3] From that time the connection between poaching and popular discontent had been strong. The Peasants' Revolt of 1381 was sparked by wage cuts and the enforcement of a poll tax. In the scare that followed the ill-fated rebellion, it was discovered that instead of attending church on Sundays and holidays, labourers and other members of the lower orders often hunted game and 'under such colours they made their assemblies, conferences and conspiracies for to rise and disobey their allegiance'.[4] To end these subversive Sunday gatherings a qualification of £40 per annum was set upon the right to hunt game,[5] which is the origin of the game laws and their long, unhappy consequences.

At the start of the seventeenth century the £40 qualification was raised to £100 and in 1671 the Game Act made it necessary to actually own land worth more than £100 a year, or to have some prospect of doing so through inheritance. A person so qualified was not limited to hunting on his own land. As one historian of eighteenth century game laws has put it:

> *For all practical purposes, the qualified sportsman could hunt where he pleased, while the unqualified sportsman could not hunt even on his own land. Thus it was that the game of England became the property not of the owner of the land on which it was found but rather of an entire social class, the English country gentleman.*[6]

In 1770 an Act was passed making anyone convicted of poaching at night liable to six months' imprisonment and one year's imprisonment with a public whipping for a second offence.[7] By 1800 the increase in poaching and the formation of well-organised gangs to supply the lucrative urban blackmarket for game, a consequence of the rise of the leisured urban middle classes with money to spend on eating out at restaurants, led to an Act designed to treat offenders as rogues and vagabonds and so liable to sentences of hard labour or impressment into the army or navy.[8] The effect was simply to stiffen the poachers' determination to resist arrest and to stimulate the formation of larger gangs. To counter this the Ellenborough Act of 1803 made it a capital felony to offer armed resistance to lawful arrest. The Act had the desired effect until the post-Napoleonic Wars recession and distress of the period after 1815 led to a doubling of poaching convictions in 1816. Parliament responded the next year with legislation for transporting convicted poachers for seven years, even if they had been unarmed at the time of the offence.[9]

Most of those arrested were rural workers and paupers who poached to survive. While poaching was not usually in itself an overt act of protest, implicit in the activity was the assumption that game was the property of all, an attitude that was part of the same complex of beliefs about common rights that informed enclosure riots,[10] gleaning disturbances and other expressions of communal discontent. This attitude also lay beneath the refusal of the rural poor to condemn poaching and those of their considerable numbers who pursued this activity. Looking down from the top of the social spectrum in 1816, one writer observed:

The property which they [the Game Laws] protect is viewed with peculiar jealousy both by those who are precluded from taking it, and those to whom its enjoyment is secured. The former consider it as a common right of which they are unjustly deprived ... [11]

A Cambridgeshire magistrate, when asked his opinion of the rural labourers' attitude to poaching, replied, 'they do not consider [it] to be a moral offence'.[12] Similar observations would also resound through the Silver Wood affair and its aftermath.

Opinions from the bottom of the social order are harder to come by, though a few examples, with their typical appeals to Biblical authority, make the point. An old labourer, quoted by Bovill in his study of English country life between 1780 and 1830, said:

A wonderful lot of working men don't believe as there's any harm in poaching. We never read that in the Testament, nor yet in the Bible. We always

read there that the wild birds is sent for the poor
man as well as the quality.[13]

The 'King of the Norfolk Poachers' expresses identical feelings in his famous autobiography:

I have always had the idea that game was as much
mine as anyone else's. Did not God say that he
gave all the beasts and birds for the use of Man,
not for the rich alone[?][14]

And the same sentiments echo through a Lincolnshire poaching ballad:

And buck and doe, believe it so.
A pheasant or an 'are,
Was sent on earth for ev'ry one
Quite equal for to share. [15]

These attitudes were common among the extensive poaching fraternity and those who benefited from their activities. The many British poaching ballads reflect the lack of moral recrimination in popular attitudes towards poaching. Most frequently the game keeper is portrayed as the villainous opponent of the bold, loyal and usually heroic poacher. The heroes are brave-hearted fellows, attacked by keepers and taken to gaol where they are cruelly beaten. In a ballad titled 'The Keepers and the Poachers',[16] the poacher is overpowered by five keepers and prefers to die rather than inform upon his comrades. The poacher's dog is wounded 'out of spite' by the keeper in another well-known song, 'The Nottingham Poacher'.[17] In 'Bill Brown', later to be printed by a local newspaper in the context of the Silver Wood poachers' trial,[18] a burning hatred leads to the dead hero's friend avenging his death at the hands of the keeper:

I dressed myself up next night in time,
I got to the woods and the clock struck nine;
The reason was and I'll tell you why,
To find the gamekeeper I'll go try,
Who shot my friend, and he shall die.

The avenger finally discovers the keeper:

Then I took my piece fast in my hand,
Resolved to fire if Tom did stand;
Tom heard the name and turned him round,
I fired and brought him to the ground;
My hand gave him his deep death wound.

Now revenge, you see, my hopes have crowned,
I've shot the man that shot Bill Brown,
Poor Bill no more these eyes will see,
Farewell, dear friend, farewell to ye,
For I've crowned his hopes and his memory.

Murdering the keeper who, as in the Silver Wood affray, was well-known to the poachers, is portrayed as justified revenge. No guilt is ascribed to Bill Brown's avenger; this is an acceptable and explicable act.

Much the same sentiments, though less extremely expressed, are found in 'The Gallant Poacher', in which a keeper also kills one member of a small poaching gang. The five remaining members of the poaching gang are imprisoned, still mourning their comrade:

It makes our hearts to mourn;
Our comrades were to prison sent,
It being our enemies' intent
that there they should remain.

But they are released and the last verse is a striking malediction against the keeper:

Now the murderous man who did him kill,
All on the ground his blood did spill,
Must wander far against his will,
And find no resting place.
Destructive things
His conscience stings;
He must wander through the world forlorn,
And ever feel the smarting thorn;
And pointed at with finger scorn,
And die in sad disgrace.

Economic hardship and the need for food often appear in the ballads as motives for poaching. But the most important characteristic of the poaching ballads is the complete absence of recrimination and the explicit justification of poaching game, sheep stealing and even murder. This popular attitude, itself an ancient one, was to play an important role in this tale. So important that it would save the neck of William Sykes.

While they may only have been, at best, dimly conscious of it, William Sykes and his poaching friends were the inheritors of this long tradition of covert common rights.[19] The need to fill the bowls and bellies of hungry children, or even just to gain a few spare coppers, was certainly the most immediate motivation for poaching. At least it was in this part of the country,[20] which had its own extensive and intense history of confrontation between those who 'owned' the game as well as the right to hunt it and those who were in need of it. But need was not the only motive. The appeal of taking something – anything – back from the estates of those who had usurped what had once been the common larder was always present. Although this attitude was not often voiced outside poaching ballads, it lay at the base of the community acceptance of poaching, even when it involved serious violence, as it had in the brief but bloody affray by Silver Wood.

2   *The Poacher's Fate*

Amidst a dead stillness the jury took their places ...

Sheffield and Rotherham Independent, 24 December 1865

After the fight in Silver Wood, Robert Woodhouse led the poachers to safety by way of Herringthorpe. There they split up and scurried back to their various lodgings by whatever routes their fear afforded them. William Sykes went home to Myra and the children, who were used to his nocturnal outings; his late returns were commonplace. Myra knew her husband would be long in returning home that night, and that he would not be coming from the pub. Calming himself William crept into bed, though it is unlikely that he got much sleep, especially as Myra had to be told of the night's misdeeds Perhaps there were long silences in the darkness between them as the potential consequences of the incident by Silver Wood sank in.

For a few days, nothing was heard. It was almost long enough for William and Myra to believe the incident had never happened. But then the *Sheffield and Rotherham Independent* published an article titled 'Desperate Encounter with Poachers near Rotherham'.[1] The article reported the incident and the inquest into the death of Lilley but claimed that the surviving keepers were unable to identify any of the poachers. At this stage few were aware that, as a known lawbreaker, Woodhouse had been routinely arrested the morning after the affray. The police searched his home and took him to be identified by keepers Machin and Butler. But they could not, or would not, swear that the burly ex-publican had been one of the desperate men in Silver Wood.

Next day, the *Sheffield Daily Telegraph* carried the news that the keepers had been well armed but the poachers had not stolen Lilley's clothing as originally thought. The article also pointed out that

> *The locality, it is known, has been for some time in previous years the resort of poachers, and within a mile or two of the place there have been several desperate encounters. About a year ago a gamekeeper was at night met by a number of marauders who assailed him most furiously with stones, and he barely escaped falling a victim to their violence.*[2]

The inquest established only the basic facts. Lilley's father, a farm labourer of Cantley, identified the body as that of his son 'who he believed was about 34 or 36 years old'. The proceedings were then adjourned to allow for a post-mortem examination.

Another local newspaper, the *Sheffield and Rotherham Advertiser* had also reported 'a savage and fatal encounter with a gang of poachers' in which

> *The poachers turned savagely on the keeper, one of them instantly felling Lilley with a hedge stake and the others kicking him savagely about the head and body as he lay helpless and insensible on the ground.*

The article went on to describe the extensive weaponry carried by Lilley, the disclosure of which 'created no small sensation' in the coroner's court. Lilley was *armed with one of those formidable weapons known as a 'knuckle-duster', a double-barrelled-pistol, loaded almost to the muzzle, and capped ready for action; and, as if these were not enough, he had in the pocket of his shooting coat a weapon almost indescribable, but in shape somewhat like the jagged ball borne by the figures of Gog and Magog in the London Guildhall. His three companions also carried pistols and other formidable weapons of offence and defence and had with them a savage retriever dog.*

The writer also made a direct connection with the origins of the game laws and their ongoing consequences, accurately noting that 'The game laws are a relic of the barbarous enactments of the Norman conquest'.[3]

In the meantime, the police, under the supervision of Detective-Inspector Hockaday of Wakefield, were sure they were on to a promising scent. Bone and Bentcliffe's dogs were well known to the keepers and these two men were brought in on the Thursday. Though he made a statement in which he claimed to have been at home at 9 o'clock on the night of the affray, the police had discovered nets and a gun at Bone's house. In his statement Bone claimed to have been unemployed for six weeks and that he was the sole breadwinner for his wife and children. 'I live as I can,' he said.

Bone denied being in Silver Wood. So did the others. Their lies bought them some time. They were released while the police continued their investigations and the inquest was adjourned for two weeks. During this short period the poachers unwisely met in the Sykes home to discuss their situation. The meeting was bitter and heated. Booth, the oldest, kept saying that the others should not 'have done so much at him' and that those whose actions had ended in Lilley's death should be the ones to 'suffer'. According to the subsequent evidence Sykes played a leading role in exhorting them all to stick together and admit nothing. Their main trump card was the fact that the surviving keepers had not, and probably would not, name the men they had fought with in the wood if they had not yet done so.

We do not know if Myra was at home during these conversations, though with four children to tend it is most likely that she was. Overhearing the raised voices, the angry swearing and the recriminations of the poachers she must have become increasingly concerned. As her later letters to William reveal, she was a worrier. She had plenty to worry about. We also know from her letters that William was not a husband who communicated often or well. In matters of such seriousness he would have been especially inclined to keep his own counsel.

While the police pursued their investigations and the poachers argued and worried, larger events were unfolding that would rapidly take control of the affair and the consequences of one moonlit night's misadventure. The consortium of gentlemen who owned the shooting rights in Silver Wood had, after Lilley's death, almost immediately posted the substantial reward of £250 for information leading to the conviction of the killer, an amount to be raised by private subscription. They also wrote to the Home Secretary requesting an additional reward be offered by the government as well as a free pardon for anyone giving information about the fight, as long as the informer was not the one who had committed the murder.

The inquest resumed on 25 October. By now the broad outlines of the incident and of the submerged local tensions beneath it were emerging. Despite some intense questioning, the keepers continued to be indifferent witnesses and were evasive in identifying the poachers: 'several of the parties concerned appear to have displayed considerable reluctance in giving any information', as the Sheffield *Daily Telegraph* put it.[4]

One inquest juryman wanted to know of the police witness if Lilley's pistol had been capped and loaded. It had been, the witness confirmed. The same juror also asked if any skin had been found on the hair attached to the hedge stake that had presumably been the murder weapon. 'No', the Constable replied stolidly, adding that the 'Coroner said he could see no traces of hair'.

Another juryman asked for the contents of the pistol to be 'drawn'. This showed that it was loaded with 70 corns of shot and only a light charge of powder, the implication being that the weapon had been loaded with the intent of causing serious damage if discharged at close range.

The head keeper, John Hawkins, appeared and stated that the keepers had 'expected poachers, because it was a likely night, and we had them before'. He was quick to point out, as did the other keepers questioned, that 'We did not know they were coming'. Hawkins also said that although he, too, had been armed with a pistol, it was only for signalling and that he did not usually carry such a weapon.

Hawkins's evidence revealed that Lilley had been a frequent associate of his and a keeper for a considerable time. There was also no love lost between the two sides of the game wars. Upon seeing the keepers that night near Silver Wood, a poacher had cried out, 'Hey up, chaps, the b——s are here.' As a local reporter observed, 'It appears that Lilley was a marked man amongst the poaching fraternity. He was the Ishmael of his calling, against whom every poacher was ready to raise his hand.'[5]

The coroner questioned Hawkins about the identity of the poachers. Despite intensive interrogation Hawkins was reluctant to name the poachers even though, as would be established at the later trial, he had grown up with Teale and known him for almost 20 years.[6] A clearly frustrated coroner declared the head keeper's answers to be unsatisfactory.

As well as their testimony, the actions of the keepers during the affray also came in for considerable scrutiny, especially those of Hawkins. A juryman asked, 'Do you really think Lilley would have been killed if you had gone to assist him?' Hawkins replied, 'He was killed before we got into the field, it is my opinion.' This, together with his perception that 'there was such a number of them', was all the defence the head keeper could muster as to why he had not gone to the assistance of the dying man. The inaccurate belief – or perhaps the convenient fabrication – that there had been between 12 or 15 poachers in the field that night was parroted in keeper Machin's evidence when it was his turn to take the stand.

Machin was also reluctant to identify the poachers. He described the man who hit Lilley as tall and stout and powerful 'in a middling way'. But if the keepers did not know who the poachers were, they certainly knew the keepers. The poacher who was hitting Lilley had said to Machin, 'It's thee, thou b——y Sheffield b——r. We have heard a deal of talk about thee, and thah shall have it nah tha has come.'

At the conclusion of his summation, Coroner John Webster handed down the verdict of 'wilful murder by several persons at present unknown'. He observed that the situation was an unhappy one and forthrightly recorded his dislike of the game laws and, presumably, of the system of privilege that brought them into being and kept them in place: 'I think it is a pity that any man should lose his life for the sake of game.' But, as he went on to say, 'Nevertheless, the game law is the law of the land'. When reminded by the lawyer for the murdered man's relations that such matters were the concern of the legislature, the coroner replied, 'Laws which cannot be maintained in their integrity, nor carried out except at the risk of killing either poachers or gamekeepers, cannot be very good laws.'

Webster echoed the views of a growing number of middle-class citizens regarding the negative consequences of the country's extensive and often draconian game laws. His distaste for his duty in this case echoed other concerns about poaching, the law and the character of those whose interests the game laws protected.

These lofty opinions also meshed closely with those held by many of the more lowly members of the local community. Poaching was not considered a crime by most of those who practised it and those who benefited from it. As one of the local newspapers pointed out, 'The police complain of the apathy on the part of the country people and tell us that the moral sense of the villagers is deadened where matters of poaching are concerned.'[7] The death of the keeper was unfortunate, of course, but he and his companions were disliked and distrusted locally and so most were inclined to treat the death as an accident or, perhaps less charitably given Lilley's reputation, as good riddance. Certainly violent death by beating and kicking was common and unremarkable in this brutal time and place, being frequently cited in cases of manslaughter and murder.

Possibly concerned that these sentiments would work against anyone being arrested for Lilley's murder, Jubb and his associates, two days after the inquest, increased the reward to the very large sum of £350, which they advertised in the newspapers and in handbills distributed through the Rotherham area.[8] The following day, the aggressive defenders of their property rights, Henry Jubb and his 'gentlemen' friends were, surprisingly, castigated along with the poachers and the keepers in the conservative *Sheffield Daily Telegraph*. There was little doubt what the *Telegraph* thought about the actions of the keepers. They should have 'gone in like men to save their gallant comrade from death, instead of sneaking away to hide in the thicket like so many pitiful curs, while the horrid work of death was going on'.

The paper pointed out that Jubb had been only too quick to post a large reward while ignoring the plight of the murdered gamekeeper's widow and seven children. With no other means of support, Mrs Lilley had been forced to seek relief from the parish. The *Telegraph* concluded with a ringing echo of what was no doubt the popular sentiment that 'The only man who behaved well in the business was the man who suffered, and as for the rest, what can we say of them except that the behaviour has been un-English on all sides – the poachers acting like savages – the keepers like hares – and the employer like a snob.'[9]

Apparently stung by such violent adverse publicity,[10] especially coming from the section of the press that could generally be relied upon to support the game laws, Jubb and his associates hastily arranged a small annual allowance for Lilley's widow and children. With all this publicity and official action of one kind and another, the case generated passionate local speculation, rumour and gossip, a good deal of which surfaced in the local newspapers, adding fuel to what the affrighted poachers were hearing from friends and relations.

As the police gradually tightened their net around the poachers, Woodhouse, Bone, Savage and Bentcliffe left the district, hoping to avoid capture. But William stayed at home with Myra and the children, relying perhaps on his earlier argument that the keepers could not identify the poachers with any certainty. But this was wishful thinking. Early in the morning of 31 October, the police pounded on the door of the Sykes home with a warrant for William's arrest. They searched the house, discovering, as they had anticipated they would, the implements of the poacher's trade, a large number of nets and pegs, sticks, a ferret and wire for fashioning snares, all stupidly stored by Sykes. But there was no murder weapon. Saying only, 'It's a bad job', the characteristically taciturn William was taken into custody amidst the tears of 11-year-old Ann and the despairing looks of Myra, young William, Alfred and Thirza.

That night and the next, in a coordinated series of raids around Sheffield, Rotherham and further afield, Bone was taken at Wakefield and Bentcliffe at Rawmarsh, where, according to the press, he was living with a woman of notorious character. Teale was lodging in Kimberworth and Booth at home in the village of New York. All were found with various incriminating items of the poaching trade. Woodhouse, the poacher with the most serious criminal record, was again detained by police but again released. It would soon be clear why.

On 2 November all the papers were able to report that the seven suspects were in custody. Woodhouse was described as about 40 years of age and 'powerful looking'. Teale, an unemployed labourer and bachelor from Cantley, was said to have harboured a grudge against Lilley because the dead keeper had once been responsible for having Teale's father convicted of some minor offence. Bone was the father of five children. Sykes was a forgeman but had not worked 'for some months'. Bentcliffe had appeared in court before. The oldest man, David Booth, was 54 and worked as a railway navvy.[11] At this stage, the police had not yet caught up with Ginger Savage.

The accused were kept in separate cells until 3 November when, dressed by the police in their poaching apparel, 'the worthy watchers of game', as they were described in the press, picked three of them out of an identification parade. Wondering why Woodhouse was not among their number, one of the poachers remarked, 'There was another to come yet.'

But there was not. The seventh poacher, Woodhouse, had turned 'approver', betraying his companions to the police. The *Sheffield Daily Telegraph* confirmed 'the pretty generally admitted fact that Woodhouse is the chief approver, or rather *the* approver, as only one can, we believe, be allowed to claim the pardon offered by the Secretary of State'.[12]

It was now clear that only six of the seven poachers would be examined for the murder of Lilley. A few days later the press reported that 'The friends of Teale, Sykes and Bone ... have displayed a rather hostile feeling towards the friends of Woodhouse, Booth and Bentcliffe, and of the first mentioned they speak in terms of almost unmeasured hatred and contempt.'[13] The same day the police rounded up Ginger Savage – *aka* Shaw, Shoden and Boden – who had legged it to his home village near Nottingham. He was drunk at the time.

On 7 November all the poachers were arraigned at Rotherham Court House. A large crowd gathered around the building. The reporter described the prisoners and was particularly struck by William Sykes, rendering his appearance in near-heroic terms that would have been surprising to most people. Sykes was good-looking, the journalist thought, though in a military way. His features were sharp, his complexion bright and he had a hard and fierce expression and an acute and restless eye. 'It is not often that a face so fitted to express endurance and scornful courage and so thoroughly martial could be found for the sculptor, and it seems a pity that a man whom nature fitted for a soldier, and whom Lord Byron would have been delighted with as an ideal corsair, should have drifted into the position of a poacher.'

Sykes was clearly edgy, but this did not prevent the journalist discerning his 'small, tightly-compressed mouth, the sharp chin, the knife-like nose, the cheekbones overhanging the lower face in a graceful curve like beetling cliffs, and the eyes peering like a pair of keen falcons from their recess beneath the arched eyebrows . . .'. The poetic reporter thought that William Sykes 'appeared to feel the humiliation of his position' and that he was 'as little at his ease as a caged eagle'.[13]

The *Rotherham and Masbrough Advertiser* was far more prosaic. After referring to the poachers as a group 'rather of a low type', the writer went on to say: 'Sykes is of moderate stature and pretty stoutly built. He is on the whole not bad looking, though his features are lowering bad and he assumes a rather mysterious and thoughtful air ... His general demeanour seems to indicate some little shyness or furtiveness.' The *Advertiser* also republished the *Telegraph*'s Byronic homily on the same page.[15]

The effusions of the unidentified *Telegraph* journalist continued in contrasting Sykes to his companions. Teale was 'long and wiry' and had 'the head of a weasel' that he 'carried on a neck which for length might be called a gizzard'. Bone was 'broad across the chest' but 'short and vulgar looking in the extreme, sallow-complexioned, pock-marked ... with a peculiarly cock-sparrowy kind of strut and possessed of little sinister eyes'. In describing the keepers Hawkins and Butler, the journalist wrote that 'Neither of the men are persons from whose look we should infer any lack of courage, though neither have that appearance of muscular strength possessed by some of the prisoners, nor yet that air of defiant belligerence and that intense power of will which distinguish Sykes.'[16]

The proceedings at this appearance were brief. The Crown pleaded the recent arrest of Savage as cause for extra preparation time and the poachers were remanded to appear again on 15 November. Then the full presentation of the prisoners would determine whether there were further, more serious, charges to answer.

The prosecution was at pains to paint Woodhouse as relatively little implicated and to show William Sykes as the man who had savagely murdered Lilley. In his opening address the prosecutor brushed aside any consideration of the inequity of the game laws as a factor in the case. Such issues would simply cloud the substance of the matters before the court. A large number of witnesses were called by the prosecution. The finding of the court was that all seven prisoners should be 'fully committed for trial at the ensuing Leeds assizes for murder'.[17]

Next morning, still in the clothes they wore on the night of the murder, the prisoners were removed from the police station. They took their leave of wives and children at the courthouse where most of the men broke down, certain they would never see their loved ones again. They were then driven by omnibus through the streets to Masborough Station as 'eager crowds congregated and displayed an ardent desire to catch a glimpse of them'. At the station a large crowd gathered to farewell the local men. The poachers were chained together, although Woodhouse was kept carefully separate from the companions he had betrayed, but together with Booth who had by then also made a statement. As they waited on the platform 'Sykes was visited by one of his little girls, who wept in a very distressing manner as she threw herself into the arms of her father'.[18] This must have been Thirza, though it was her older sister Ann who would come to feel her father's absence most keenly in the coming years. As Myra would later write to William in Western Australia:

Ann is the worst of them all about it and She is bothered greatly About it every day in hir life ...

That day the newspaper also reported that Mr Jubb and 'one or two gentlemen' had raised 'a small sum' to be given to Booth's wife and large family of youngsters. This would allow her to buy 'a basket of smallware for hawking, that having been a pursuit she followed previous to her marriage, or if sufficient funds are raised a small shop may be stocked'.

Lilley's murder and the subsequent proceedings were exciting intense speculation. Local newspapers devoted columns and columns of finely-spaced newsprint to the particulars of the case, reporting in detail on what was said, what was done and what was rumoured. On a number of occasions two to three broadsheet-page summaries of events were published, keeping readers abreast of the news as well as keeping them in anticipation of the upcoming trial at the Leeds winter assizes in late December.

It would be almost two months before the case was heard in court. During that time the politics and prejudices of local class conflict ground on. There was gossip among the red-brick rows, in the ironworks, down the mines and in the pubs about who had struck the blow or blows that killed Lilley. William Sykes's family mostly followed the lead of his elder brother John, a well-to-do carpenter. Like him, they had moved into more exalted social settings and were torn between concern for their youngest member and the stigma that his actions and the consequences of them might bring. Myra's family, the less economically resilient Wilcocks, shrugged their shoulders and maintained a sympathetic distance.

That, at least, is the impression that comes through the lines of Myra's letters and what little is told in the official records. The Henry Jubbs of the world were keen to see justice done so that their 'rights' were publicly vindicated, while the increasing numbers of middle-class opponents of the game laws hoped that the trial would provide yet another example – should one be needed – of the absurdity and inequity of usurping the ownership of wild animals.

3 Common Folk and Common Rights

The prisoner Mason addressed the Court as champion of the rights of the poor, whose property he said the commons were. The judge stated distinctly to the prisoners and the jury, that the poor had no such right.

Trial of an anti-enclosure activist, 1815

'Sykes' is an old and widespread name in Yorkshire, with noted and eminent bearers scattered through its industrial and cultural history. But William Sykes, puddler and poacher, was not one of these worthies. Obscurely born in 1827 his fate was to grow up and live a not so good part of his adult life in the manufacturing cauldron of the Sheffield–Rotherham conurbation. It was a place of coal mines and ironworks, shrouded in the stink, smoke and noise of the Industrial Revolution grinding into high gear. Almost all those of William Sykes's station could look forward only to a life bounded by the pits, the works and the manifold dangers of barely bridled exploitation.

Myra[1] Wilcock, destined to be William's wife, was born five years later into similar circumstances and limited expectations. Both were members of large families, an almost inevitable feature of life at that time. William had two brothers and three sisters. Myra had four brothers and two sisters. Another reality of the time and place was that both William's and Myra's mothers were widowed early, probably through industrial accidents. William's father had been a coachman and Myra's a coal miner. William was not yet 14 when his father died; Myra would have barely remembered hers. Both the Sykes and Wilcock families lived just outside Greasborough, at Far Green.

As they grew up, living not far from each other but seemingly not meeting until their teens, Myra and William felt the full force of industrialism and its attendant ills. During the eighteenth century, there had been vast enclosures of common land, as usual to the benefit of a privileged few who had an eye for and the means to exploit the wealth above and below the ground. This part of the county was a noted hotbed of social dissatisfaction and political disturbance, which culminated in the Great Charter of 1832. The Reform Bill that arose from the effective actions of the Chartists enfranchised many workers for the first time and also created two members of parliament for Sheffield. Despite this early success, political agitation continued throughout the 1830s and into the 1840s. While there is no evidence that William or Myra were directly involved in political agitation of any kind,[2] their lives were touched by these attempts to better the lot of the working class as much as they were tarnished by the consequences of industrialism.

After the death of William Sykes senior his widow, Thirza, took the fatherless family home to the village of Greasbrough. The year was 1841. Together with his brothers John and Joshua, and sisters Emma, Rebecca and Elizabeth, William soon gained a new father. He was a man named Gascoigne, probably a miner. Whether this new arrangement was a happy one we cannot tell, but we do know that William was himself soon gouging black fuel from far beneath the ground alongside other sweating miners, many even younger than his 14 years.

Some of the children employed – or condemned – to the pits at this time were as young as four years old. So poorly were they treated that a commission was established in 1840 to investigate the conditions of child labour in mines and factories throughout the country. The commission's findings, published in 1842, told a harrowing tale of misery, squalor, degradation, abuse and virtual enslavement. Unfavourable comparisons were made with the conditions of slaves on West Indian plantations. The legislation that eventuated from the report, while considerably watered down in the House of Lords, many of whose members had a financial interest in perpetuating cheap child labour, banned the employment of children under 10 in coal mines.

Yorkshire featured strongly in the commission's report, especially in relation to unsafe work practices and the provision of insufficient and poor quality nutrition for children who often worked between 11 and 14 hours a day. The children, male and female, were generally employed as trappers, ensuring that the ventilation of the pits worked as efficiently as such primitive mechanisms allowed. Sarah Gooder, aged eight, told the commission: 'I'm a trapper in the Gawber pit. It does not tire me, but I have to trap without light, and I'm scared. Sometimes I sing when I have a light, but not in the dark; I dare not sing then. I don't like being in the pit.'[3]

Coal had been mined in Yorkshire since at least the thirteenth century and at Greasbrough before 1700. But even as late as the 1820s the area was described in *Baines's*

Yorkshire[4] as 'a small village, pleasantly situated on a delightful eminence; its inhabitants generally consist of farmers and miners'. The population was reckoned at 1252. The village was eight miles from Sheffield and two miles north of Rotherham. At this time Rotherham was also merely 'a small market town' with two principal inns and a population of just over 3500. Its market was on Mondays, with every second Monday a fair 'for horned cattle'. On 1 December there was a fair for 'horses, horned cattle, sheep, &c.',[5] with a Whit Monday fair as well.

This pleasant-sounding balance of the rural and the proto-industrial was, even as the gazetteers made these observations, undergoing profound change. 'The town is far from elegant', noted one such writer in the early 1820s. 'The streets are narrow, and irregular; and the houses have, in general, a dull and dingy appearance.' Already the industry that would define this area was in development: 'A considerable trade is here carried on in coals, and in other articles, by means of the river Don.'[6]

Just across the valley in iron-ore rich Masborough, Samuel Walker had founded his ironworks in the mid-eighteenth century. The radical Tom Paine had worked here while the factory was casting the iron bridge Rennie threw across the Thames and is said to have written his *Age of Reason* (1790) during this period. By the 1820s Walker's could be described as 'one of the most extensive and flourishing establishments of the kind in Europe'.[7]

By the time the Sykes family moved back to Greasbrough in 1841, the whole area was well on the way to becoming a vast industrial landscape, pocked with coal mines, forges and steam hammers. Nearby Sheffield was described by a traveller in 1843 as 'one of the dirtiest and smoky towns I ever saw'. The town was hilly and the smoke from the 'quantity of small forges without tall chimneys' hung in the streets. While the children often washed themselves before bed, 'their bodies imbibe continual dust and grime' and people lived in an atmosphere in which they continually breathed in smoke and soot.[8]

At 24 years of age, William Sykes had, by 1851, considerable experience of living and working in this landscape and was employed in one of the local pits as a coal trammer, pushing tubs of coal from the face to the central collection point. He was the last of his siblings to marry and, perhaps motivated by that knowledge, began to court Myra Wilcock who was working as a domestic servant at the Ashcroft Academy, Wentworth, a boarding school for young gentlemen. Even for that era it was a drawn-out courtship. It was not until two years later that they married at the parish church of Sheffield. In accordance with the working-class affectation of the time, both bride and groom signed the register with an 'X' even though both had received basic schooling and were – just – able to read and write, as the evidence of their letters and other documents shows. Myra was 21.

Soon after Myra and William were married, children began to arrive. Ann was born in 1854, Alfred in 1857 and Thirza in 1859. When the fourth child, William, arrived six years later,[9] the Sykes family moved to Midland Road, Masborough, where they lived in a standard two-up, two-down terraced house. By now William had escaped the pits. At the Masborough ironworks on the opposite side of the street he now puddled pots of molten metal preparatory to their being poured and beaten into whatever shapes and sizes had been ordered by the incessant demands of the

Sheffield–Rotherham steel industries. Hard and dangerous though puddling was, it was better than crawling through a dark coal mine and William Sykes could consider himself to have improved at least a little upon his initial lot in life.

According to *Murray's Hand-Book of Yorkshire*, Masborough was now a town of the same size as nearby Rotherham.[10] Like many other villages in this area, though, it retained something of its rural character. Despite the noise, stink and industrial discipline of the works that permeated every aspect of life, it was still quite easy to walk a mile or two and be out into the open country. Distinctions between city and country were more apparent than real. The factories and foundries of industry had been sucking in labour from the countryside for only a generation or so. Many people still lived their lives in villages, or in what had been villages before being engulfed by the blackened cities. From these villages or the hasty housing developments thrown up around them, workers lived a dual existence, working in the urban forges and factories for wages while retaining the habits and interests of country life during whatever leisure time they could get. Unfortunately, most of those once common lands now belonged to someone else.

The long and unhappy history of rural enclosure and appropriation of common rights had nearly reached its conclusion at this time and in this place. Inexorably, fields, footpaths and forests had all fallen into private hands intent on exploiting the resources they contained, or those that could be erected upon them, to the full. The ancient rights of common, of grazing stock, of fishing, of collecting firewood and other basic necessities of everyday life had almost entirely disappeared. Now, the fields were fenced and hedged, the fishing rights belonged to the landowners and the woods were the source of both lumber and fuel for the furnaces of the industrial revolution. 'Improving', rational agrarian progress, was the mood of the times and of those who called its tunes.

Common rights were a complex combination of legal and customary rights, privileges and obligations that often originated in the mediaeval era, or even earlier. Despite the existence of legislation, such as the Statute of Artificers (1563), that supposedly regulated work hours and conditions, there was little standardisation or complementarity between these rights and obligations. A fair day's work in one parish was longer or shorter than that in a neighbouring parish. The widespread perquisites known as 'rights of common' were equally varied and of dubious legal status. These included such things as common of pastures (the right to take the produce of the land), common of turbary (the right to cut turf for fuel), common of estovers (the right to cut wood for fuel) and common of piscary (the right to fish in someone else's waters). In some parts of the country there were also common rights of fowling and of cutting hay on common land 'according to the custom of the manor'.[11] Throughout England and Wales the local landholders and owners were bound by such precedents that might also regulate the rent they could charge and such details as the length and conditions of leases. Imperfect and unbalanced as this moral order was, it struggled on as the main mode of economic and political relationships for centuries.

By the middle of the eighteenth century this 'moral economy', as the historian Edward Thompson called it, with its assumptions of reciprocity, paternalism and deference in return for a reasonable guarantee that the necessities of life would be provided to the powerless by the powerful, was in serious decline. It had become an anachronism at the centres of power, which now preferred to encourage the normal operation of supply and demand in a free market rather than to leave things to the tinkerings of the local squire. The old assumptions were under serious challenge from the new approach of rational rural capitalism, with its emphasis on efficiency, productivity, exploitation and even morality. These innovations and the benefits they would bring to those who made them were summed up in the aims of the Board of Agriculture's 'Plan for Reprinting the Agricultural Surveys' of 1795:

> *Perhaps the following is the most natural order for carrying on such important investigations; namely to ascertain,*
> 1. *The riches to be obtained from the surface of the national territory.*
> 2. *The mineral or subterraneous treasures of which the country is possessed.*
> 3. *The wealth to be derived from its streams, rivers, canals, inland navigations, coasts and fisheries: And*
> 4. *The means of promoting the improvements of the people in regard to their health, industry, and morals, founded on a statistical survey, or a minute and careful enquiry into the actual state of every parochial district in the kingdom, and the circumstances of its inhabitants ...* [12]

The increasing disparities between the economic rationalising of industrial capitalism and the values hanging over from the agrarian past created long-lasting and serious social conflict. From Elizabethan times onwards, the enclosing of previously common land, woods, streams and other natural resources by private owners was the source of fierce resistance. Enclosure went to the heart of the moral order of deference and paternalism that kept the rural poor alive before industrialisation. It expropriated their physical access to resources and it outraged the customary expectations of what was right and fair.

A terse exchange between the judge and a man accused, with four others, of breaking down the fences of a Norfolk enclosure in 1815 gives a hint of popular attitudes and shows the gap that existed between the rulers and the ruled. Similar sentiments were to be voiced in the proceedings of William Sykes's trial for murder:

> *The prisoner Mason addressed the Court as champion of the rights of the poor, whose property he said the commons were. The judge stated distinctly to the prisoners and the jury, that the poor had no such right as was asserted by the prisoner Mason.* [13]

While the hapless Mason was deluded, it was a delusion he shared with millions of other English people at this time.

There were many other outbreaks of resistance to the expropriation of ways of life and livelihoods through enclosure. Some were small instances of local people simply 'possessioning' or circling a piece of land that they believed should be available to all rather than just to the exploitation of the fortunate or crafty few. One earlier case involved Charles I who enclosed Richmond Park with a high wall, to the great displeasure of the people of several adjoining parishes. The parishioners, on a number of occasions into the eighteenth century, 'beat the bounds' and pulled down the wall to register their protest at this royal affront and, in vain, to assert their customary rights.[14]

Other enclosure-related struggles were bitter and violent confrontations between two incompatible ways of seeing the world, as in the Hampshire forest of Waltham during the 1720s. Here, there were prolonged episodes of ritualised deer poaching by locals, who blacked their faces in the traditional disguise of the rural rioter. Deer were taken, trees, fish, ponds and fences – the trappings of agrarian exploitation – were destroyed by hammer, fire and knife. Such was the scale of this protest that the authorities came to see it, hysterically, as a potential Jacobite uprising. In 1723 the Waltham Black Act was enacted, under which deer stealers who went armed and with blackened faces were liable to the death penalty.[15]

More than a century later, on 6 September 1830 at Otmoor in Oxfordshire, 1000 people circled the boundaries of the moor that had been enclosed 15 years before, thereby formally possessioning it, as they said had been their habit in the past.[16] There were continuing enclosure riots throughout East Anglia, especially notable outbursts being in 1817, 1825, 1826 and 1844. There were protests against the impounding of stock by local pindars, or bailiffs. There were gleaning riots and stonings of farmers who refused to allow locals their customary perquisite of collecting leftover stubble from the fields after harvesting.

Enclosure was as much a burning issue around Rotherham and Sheffield. As elsewhere in the country throughout the eighteenth century and into the nineteenth, there had been continued and bitter resistance to the enclosure of local commons.[17] It was still an issue in 1879, when there was strong community opposition to the enclosure of Maltby Common.[18] A locally – and pseudonymously – published history was still fulminating against the appropriation of common lands as late as 1907[19] and private encroaching on public rights of way still has the power to generate intense controversy in Britain.

But most of these protests were hopeless causes. The economic rationalism that underpinned the new industrialism eroded the traditional assumptions of common rights upon which large numbers of people depended for their very existence. By the early nineteenth century the gentry was increasingly inclined to ignore the niceties of tradition and custom in favour of the more profitable practices of economic rationalism and public order.

Sykes and his friends were fringe dwellers between the city and the country. But like the prisoner Mason, the Waltham Blacks and the Otmoor possessioners, they were also caught between a rural past with its now archaic assumptions of a social and economic compact between the rulers and the ruled and the individualist, 'improving' industrial present. William and his comrades were no strangers to secret woodland ways, dark nights and outwitting gamekeepers. But they earned their daily bread, and that of their usually large families, sweating in the furnaces of the steel industry and lived in villages that were rapidly becoming suburbs.

These village suburbs frequently preserved the core symbols of rural life in the form of the church, the village green – often the only common land left – and the usual collection of inns or public houses. Around this focus, the rows of cramped red-brick terraces marched relentlessly out into the surrounding countryside, year after year. Thrown up in a hurry and with little thought given to planning or amenities, the suburbs developed, in fits and starts, the features that would come to typify everyday English life for the following century or more.

If there was a village church or churches, well and good. These soon became islands of piety and morality surrounded by seas of red brick. They could often be the focus of family and community life, if only for the rites of passage necessary for birth, marriage and death. The church, or more particularly the man who looked over it, was also often the only point of contact with the government and its bureaucracy. The vicar was a member of the respectable classes of society, educated, relatively well off and, at least to the likes of the Sykes and their peers, influential. It was to be St Mary's church in Greasbrough that would perform many of these functions for Myra and her family in the hard years ahead.

The church also provided the charity and scraps of education that were the lot of the working classes for much of the nineteenth century. This source of knowledge was supplemented to some extent by the secular offerings of the Mechanics' Institutes. Establishments selling the few necessities and the even-fewer indulgences available also sprang up. The matches, candles, needles, thread and other such articles that were often the treasured possessions of the urban working family were bought in dingy shops, cramped into the front room of a terrace house, or from a ramshackle lean-to built alongside.

At the opposite end of the scale from the houses of God were what the temperate and the excessively pious called 'houses of sin'. The public house was at least as important an institution in the urban villages as the church. It provided alcohol, of course, but almost as necessarily, for men at least, a place to meet, smoke, gamble and discuss the events of the time and the trivia of everyday working life. Pubs were often noisy, always smoky places where men laughed, swore, cursed and sometimes made silly threats and hatched even sillier plots.

William Sykes and his friends often met at Masborough's Black Bull Inn to drink, smoke and talk about the way things were and about how they might make some things at least a little better for themselves. The landlord, James Woolhouse, gave evidence that 'they have all been in the habit of frequenting my house'.[20] It was at the Black Bull where they had made the fateful decision to go poaching in Silver Wood. The events that followed from that simple discussion were to banish William Sykes to the other end of the Earth.

4

On Trial for Murder

He removed the muscles and exposed a comminuted fracture of the left side of the skull cap, eight or nine broken pieces being driven in upon the brain.

Mr Henry John Knight, surgeon, on the autopsy of Lilley

The poachers' trial began in Leeds a few days before Christmas. By now local interest in the affair was profound. The proceedings were reported at length and in detail by the local press. Sykes, Teale, Savage, Bone, Bentcliffe and Booth stood in the dock, sombre and attentive. But their seventh companion, William's mate Robert Woodhouse, was in the box as a witness for the prosecution.

Arrested in Sheffield at the same time as the others, Woodhouse had evidently decided the game was up and that he might as well have the large reward and save himself as well. He made a statement incriminating his companions, especially Bone, Bentcliffe, Teal and Sykes. There was a considerable amount of legal argumentation in which Woodhouse further incriminated the others, even though, as he admitted, he had been the last to leave the prostrate and dying Lilley and had struck him with his own stick, though only to see if he was still alive. Mr Campbell Foster for the accused sought to throw the guilt back onto Woodhouse, a tactic that scored as well with the jury as it did with the locals observing the trial. But it had no impact on the judge. Foster also revealed Woodhouse's criminal past in connection with poaching and suggested that he was influenced in his decision to turn approver by the large rewards that had been posted after the death of Lilley.

Most of the witnesses from the committal hearing were recalled and re-examined. It was clear that there had been a good deal of animosity between the local keepers and the poachers and that the events of the fatal night were more than random. According to head keeper Hawkins, Silver Wood was a poor area for game. This begged the obvious question of why seven experienced poachers had travelled several hours to hunt there.[1] It also raised the question of how Hawkins and the other heavily-armed keepers just happened to be in the same location that evening and had lain uncomfortably in wait there for some hours before the poachers arrived. The reluctance of Hawkins and the other keepers to identify the poachers again became an issue.

This time the judge, Justice Shee, took up the question with Hawkins directly, questioning him intensively about his relationship with Teale. The interrogation revealed that Hawkins had known Teale, boy and man, for nearly 20 years. 'And,' asked the judge incredulously, 'do you mean to say that when you left the field you did not know it to be him?' When Hawkins insisted he did not recognise Teale the judge pointed out that he had admitted meeting the accused man and having a conversation with him barely more than six months earlier. But Hawkins still insisted that he had not known it was Teale until he had seen him at Rotherham Court House.[2]

The trial progressed to the giving of medical evidence. Mr Henry John Knight, the surgeon, described in medical detail the state of Lilley after the savage attack upon him. At two in the morning of 11 October, Knight had attended Lilley. He was

> *lying on his back in bed perfectly insensible. His breathing was sterterous [sic]. He was bleeding from the head. The pupils of his eyes were fully dilated ... There was a pulpy swelling over the left temple, a lacerated wound about half an inch in extent behind the left ear, higher than this on the same side a contused and lacerated wound, starred or cross-shaped, on the top of the head there were two lacerated wounds, each about two inches in length, and there were also two lacerated wounds at the back of the head, a lacerated angular wound above the right ear, and a contused and lacerated wound on the right ear, itself dividing the cartilage [sic] of the ear.*

The doctor never saw Lilley alive again and on the following day conducted the post-mortem examination.

> *There was extravasation of blood in the left temporal muscle corresponding to the pulpy swelling, also extravasculation of blood in the whole of the muscles on the left side of the head. He removed the muscles and exposed a comminuted fracture of the left side of the skull cap, eight or nine broken pieces being driven in upon the brain. He then removed the skull cap, and in the outer membrane of the brain he found a rent about an inch in length, corresponding in position to the starred wound on the left side. Beneath this rent there was a layer of coagulated*

blood, on removing which he found the substance of the brain lacerated to about an inch in circumference. He then removed the brain and found a layer of coagulated blood at the base of the skull extended as far as the roof of the nose on the left aside and round the bones of the skull to the right side. Altogether there were eight wounds and a swelling. He attributed death to pressure upon the brain, caused by the fracture and extravasations of blood ... There were wounds behind the right and left ear that appeared to have been produced by stones.

On being cross-examined by the defence, the doctor said he found no bruising elsewhere on the body, specifically stating that 'a blow on the inside of the left leg of sufficient force to cause the deceased to roll over would leave a mark', thus contradicting Woodhouse's assertion that he had used his stick on Lilley in this way.[3]

There was further legal argument over the admissibility of Booth's statement, which confirmed much of what Bentcliffe claimed and clearly incriminated Bone, Teale and Sykes. Booth did not expect to receive any reward for his statement, saying, 'I expect to receive the benefit in another world.' He said that Teale, Bone and Sykes threatened to swear that Booth killed Lilley if he informed. 'Sykes has been very bitter about it, and said that if anyone told about it he would swear it on them.' Booth also gave another insight into the clandestine underworld of the poachers and keepers, saying that 'Teale said, I believe he swore, that if he had known it was Lilley he would not have left him so long as there had been a bit of breath in him.'

After two days of proceedings Mr Justice Shee spent nearly three hours summing up. The basic message of his summation was that the jury should find the defendants guilty of murder. When he had finished, one juror asked if there were not a verdict for them to consider against the informer. When the judge replied that Woodhouse was not in the dock, the juror was heard to mutter what most people in the court were thinking: 'I wish he was.' The jury foreman then had to explain to Justice Shee that the jury was very unhappy at not being able to render a verdict against Woodhouse. Exasperated by this display of local intransigence, the judge sent the sullen jury to consider their verdict against the accused.

It looked very bad for the poachers, especially for William Sykes. His friend Woodhouse had betrayed him and the others. Woodhouse's evidence had been carefully crafted to slide culpability away from himself and onto the others. But it was William Sykes who Woodhouse singled out for most of the blame. According to his evidence Sykes had led the poachers, he had given the warning cry when the keepers came upon them and he was the one who had to be prevented from attacking Butler in the same way he had laid into Lilley. Worst of all though, Woodhouse claimed that when he remonstrated with Sykes about attacking a man so savagely, Sykes had replied that he 'hoped the —— would die'.[4]

The poachers' defence attempted to undermine this damning evidence. Campbell Foster had pointed out that it could just as easily have been Woodhouse who struck the fatal blow as he was the last to leave the shattered Lilley on that desperate night. Antagonistic towards the informer, the jury was clearly impressed by these arguments. But most of the other evidence, together with the determination of the judge to have a verdict of murder, painted a very grim picture for the defendants. They waited fearfully for the jury's verdict.

Their trepidation was mercifully brief. The jury returned to the court in less than an hour. Either in fear or anticipation, all present expected to hear a verdict of guilty. William Sykes looked very anxious and Teale was 'visibly agitated'.

The Clerk of Arraigns: gentleman of the jury, have you agreed upon your verdict?

One of the jurors replied 'no'. But the foreman insisted 'We have.'

The Clerk of Arraigns: Do you find John Teale guilty or not guilty?

At this point the foreman of the jury declared himself too disgusted with his fellow jurors to deliver the verdict. A juror, presumably the one who had just spoken, gave the verdict of 'guilty' – then, after a cruel few seconds pause – 'of manslaughter'.

The reporter attending for the *Independent* wrote that 'The last word took the whole Court by surprise. Everybody stared incredulously at the jury, the prisoner Teale being clearly unable to believe his ears.'

The same verdict was recorded for Bone and Sykes, with Bentcliffe being recommended to mercy. Booth and Savage were found not guilty and removed from the bar.

The four convicts showed themselves to be thoroughly conscious of the vast change that had taken place in their position and prospects. The shadow of the gallows, the 'grim presence' ... was

*removed and they seemed to be indifferent as to
what fate may now be in store for them.*

Clearly astonished, 'Mr Justice Shee ... did not
disguise his dissatisfaction at the verdict of the jury for
the minor offence'.[5] He rebuked the jury for deciding
against his summing-up, his annoyance stinging the
foreman to turn and say to the juror who had delivered
the verdict: 'There! I told you how it would be.'

When these extraordinary exchanges between the
representative of the rulers and those they ruled came to
an end, the judge gave Bone and Bentcliffe 20 years
penal servitude apiece and sentenced Sykes and Teale to
life. There was a scream from among the spectators as
Bentcliffe's wife, either from relief or shock, fainted.

The toughened *Independent* reporter was also
surprised: 'The jury were obviously disconcerted by his
Lordship's observations, which were more pointed and
severe than any we have previously heard a judge
address to a jury, in the course of a pretty large
experience.' He subsequently interviewed a member of
the jury who told him that 'ten or eleven of them had
made up their minds in the course of the previous night
to a verdict of manslaughter. They refused to take the
law from a judge, who told them in express terms that
there was no element in the case that could reduce it to
manslaughter.'[6]

Why had the majority of the jurors 'refused to take
the law from a judge'? Once again, the *Independent's*
journalist provides a perceptive interpretation.

*In the first place we may take into account the
almost universal prejudice against the game laws,
which often induces juries to take a very lenient*

view of the consequences which result sometimes to the poachers or the gamekeepers through a fight over the body of a hare or a pheasant. The approver, Woodhouse, was hated by all. A universal shudder agitated the court when the wretch admitted that he used his bludgeon upon the prostrate body of Lilley, and the reason he gave for the act – that he 'wanted to see if he was moveable' – deepened the horror and aversion with which he inspired the court.

Woodhouse's prominent part in the organisation and leadership of previous poaching sorties and his admission that he informed to save his own neck had not endeared him to the jury. Nor did the fact that he was prepared to see his companions hang and to walk away with the reward money. In addition, Woodhouse had been the last to leave Lilley's body and the medical evidence showed that the blow he had given to it had not been to the leg as he claimed, but may well have been the *coup de grâce*. Added to this was the repulsion at the number, variety and unpleasantness of the weapons with which the keepers had armed themselves that night. The teaser was particularly loathsome and brutal. Even though the weapons had not been used, the intention of the keepers was clear to all.

Hovering between these lines from the newspaper accounts are the deep local tensions that lay beneath the fight at Silver Wood, tensions that can be glimpsed at certain moments during the committal and trial proceedings: the reluctance of the keepers to identify the poachers to the police, even to the judge at the committal, the fact that at least some of those involved had long associations of one kind or another and that there were considerable personal and other antagonisms between them. Hardly anyone in the community from which William Sykes and his companions came believed that there was anything wrong with poaching, apart from getting caught. And, of course, many people were of the opinion that Lilley got what he deserved.

But not everyone. On 11 November some verses were published by the *Rotherham Advertiser* that put the point of view of the gamekeepers and their supporters:

A FEW LINES ON THE MURDER OF WILLIAM LILLEY, GAMEKEEPER, OF WICKERSLEY

At Wickersely there lived a gamekeeper
Of honour and great fame
He took delight in the dead of night,
Preserving of his game.

On the tenth night of October he left his wife and
    children,
The weather was cold and chilly;
The poachers shed the blood near Silverwood
Of famous William Lilley.

It was Sykes, Teale, and Bone fought with
    hedgestakes, sticks and stones,
More like savages in a melee;
They shed the blood near Silverwood
Of famous William Lilley.

The murderers found no resting place,
Wherever they did scout;
And Hockaday from Wakefield came,
And searched the villains out.

The crime of murder will stick close to them,
Wherever they may be,
And stain the spot they finish at last –
On the gallows tree.

Though years and centuries may pass away,
Then human blood will chill
To hear the tale of wilful murder
Of poor Lilley of the hill.

Poor Lilley is gone, and we greet [mourn] him,
Though in these woods we will meet no more;
Still we hope some day to meet him
On some peaceful, happy shore.

Self-appointed judge, jury and executioner, the poet – identified only as 'H.W.' – was expressing the passions of the gamekeepers and their masters. Lilley was now a hero to that group and Sykes and his companions the bloody villains who must suffer appropriate punishment. But despite this deep enmity in one, obviously small, sector of the local community, William Sykes and his companions had beaten the very considerable odds against them. They would not hang, though perhaps their fates and those of their families would be, in some ways, worse.

Myra and William were allowed only a few brief minutes together. We can imagine what passed between them. In one of her later letters Myra would recollect how she felt at the time. William's hands felt soft and he seemed very young-looking: 'my hart Broke neley' she wrote.

Then William was led away. Myra returned home to Masborough, the children and Christmas without a father or a husband.

Only a few weeks later, Myra was back in the Leeds assizes as a witness in the night poaching case. While the poachers had been found not guilty of murdering Lilley, Booth, Savage and William Sykes still had to face the potentially serious consequences that could arise from a charge of poaching at night. The three were at the bar again little more than a week after New Year, on 9 January 1866.

5 *Another Trial*

The second trial began on a Tuesday, again before Mr
Justice Shee, and with an ironic twist. William Sykes,
now dressed in prison uniform, was acquitted before the
proceedings began and admitted as an approver against
Woodhouse who was also present as a spectator in the
court. It seems that William was not required to give
evidence in this trial, though Myra's role was to be an
important one.

In order to prove the guilt or otherwise of Booth and
Savage it was necessary to establish who had been
present at the Sykes house prior to the poaching
expedition. Myra appeared for the prosecution to point
the finger at Booth and Savage. But she also used the
opportunity to cast further doubt – if any were needed –
upon the motives of Woodhouse in approving against his
former comrades.

By now local opinion about the Silver Wood affray
and its participants had set firm. There was not much
sympathy for the keepers, including Lilley. The Judas
Woodhouse almost certainly struck the fatal blow but
had saved himself and gained the very large reward at the
expense of his mates. Now Booth and Savage, who had
allied themselves with Woodhouse's evidence against
Sykes and the others, were generally reviled. These

tensions, together with Mr Justice Shee's antagonisms, gave the trial an especially bitter edge.

The evidence turned upon interpretations of statements made by and against the poachers before the first trial for murder and as evidence during that trial. Booth was the poacher with the most to lose if it went against him, while Ginger Savage had played only a relatively minor part in what occurred.

Once again the events of the fatal night were recounted: after the poachers had bagged three rabbits and a hare they had been set upon by the keepers, led by the unfortunate Lilley. Although the trial was concerned with the comparatively minor offences of night poaching, going armed and assault, the unresolved issues of the murder trial cast their influence over the proceedings, which were largely hijacked by the question of who had murdered Lilley.

Myra was called early and gave evidence for the prosecution. She confirmed that Booth and Savage had been at her house on the night of 10 October and that they had left about 8 o'clock. 'Next day I was going to Kimberworth for my husband's nets, and met Booth and Woodhouse. Woodhouse said "Yon man's dead." I said "Who?" and Woodhouse replied 'The keeper we met last night." I said "Oh dear." Booth said nothing and only laughed.'

There was then some conversation about whether the growing number of people who knew about the incident would inform. Woodhouse was concerned about Booth's wife, but Booth scoffed at the suggestion, saying, 'Bloody likely. My wife has known me do things before, many a year since, and she has not told yet.'

Under cross-examination Myra said the powerfully

built Woodhouse told her he had given Lilley 'blows that would have killed a horse' and that he did not seem surprised to learn Lilley had died from his wounds. She then said, 'I never knew my husband guilty of being concerned in an affair of this sort. I know my husband has been sentenced to penal servitude for life ...' She broke off there and was asked another question by the solicitor: 'He was a good husband?' 'Well,' Myra replied, 'he was my husband.'

The solicitor suggested that Myra hoped her court appearance would mitigate William's situation – 'You would like to get him out?', he asked. 'I should like to hear tell of it,' Myra replied spiritedly. In further cross-examination Myra said the police had suggested to her that it would 'ease her mind' to tell what she knew in court. The questioner persisted with his suggestions that she had only come to help her husband. 'I should like to get him out if I could,' Myra admitted, 'but I am not aware that what I can say will diminish his punishment. I have told the police, because I thought it only right that murderers worse than my husband should be punished ... I think it nothing but proper that the man who said he had given strokes that would kill a horse should be punished.'

Then the solicitor asked Myra if she expected her husband's sentence to be commuted as a result of her evidence. 'No,' she replied, 'I'm told that tickets of leave are abandoned.' Then Booth, clearly incriminated by Myra's evidence, accused Myra and William of conspiring: 'Have not you and your husband not made it up between you in this very place to get us punished for it?'

Myra denied this. 'Nothing of the kind.' But Booth persisted with his suggestion that she and William had concocted this story in the brief time the husband and wife had been together after the last trial. 'I know you did when you were alone.' But Myra stoutly refuted the suggestion. 'We were not alone, there were three policemen there.' Unable to resist a joke at the expense of the police and the hostile witness, Booth said, 'And no doubt they made it up with you.' The court laughed at this but Myra stuck to her guns, saying, 'We never said anything of the kind.' At this point a female voice was heard from the public gallery crying out, 'Speak the truth, Mrs Sykes.'

On that mixed note of mirth and derision, Myra's evidence ended. She had done her best. She had stood up on behalf of her husband, even though her evidence hinted that William was less than the perfect spouse. She had also amplified the possibility that Woodhouse bore much more than a small share of the guilt that had gaoled her husband for life. Mr Shee would not miss these inferences during the remainder of the trial.[1]

Proceedings began again on Wednesday morning. By now the judge had come around to the side of local opinion about Woodhouse. During legal argument over the admissibility of Booth's statement, Mr Shee made the remarkable observation that 'I cannot understand why in the world this evidence was not taken and Woodhouse put in the dock, for he was clearly the worst of the whole lot – a thousand times.' And later, 'It is a lamentable thing indeed that we cannot admit these scraps of evidence, that we must refuse them. Here is everybody in the district, everybody all around the place and the whole district, here is everybody speaking of this as a murder, and when it comes here there is no murder at all!'

As the prosecution began summing up the judge interrupted, still unhappy at Woodhouse's absence from the dock. He asked if Woodhouse were in the court. On finding that he was the judge asked him to enter the witness box. Once there, Justice Shee questioned the informer he had just maligned about the sticks that were used during the attack. He wanted to know if Woodhouse's stick was there among the exhibits. It was not, but the judge asked, 'Were they all as thick as these?' Woodhouse replied, 'Yes, some of them rather thicker', apparently not realising the judge's intention to reinforce for the jury the fact that Woodhouse had been carrying a stick at least as deadly as those of the other poachers.

After this singular intervention from the bench, defending counsel continued his final address to the jury, suggesting that Myra's bias actually supported rather than undermined Booth's case. He congratulated her for coming forward and exposing herself to being 'compelled to admit that the wife of the prisoner Booth was a much more respectable person than she was'.

This attempt to blacken Myra's character would be specifically addressed by the judge in his summing-up. He thought the suggestion that Myra was trying to influence the jury in favour of William unlikely and that 'the questions put to her on that point were all very properly answered'.

The judge, now in accord with local sympathies, had clearly developed an aversion to Woodhouse. He returned to this theme again during his summing-up when he called Woodhouse 'a good-for-nothing man' and stated, 'You cannot rely on what a man like that says.' The judge said he disliked Woodhouse particularly 'because he was in a superior position to the other men, a sub-contractor, and the very man who ought to be the first to prevent them doing a wickedness of that kind'.

And a little later: 'Woodhouse came before them as bad an accomplice as ever made his appearance before the jury.' He went on to cite Myra's testimony as possibly incriminating Woodhouse in perjury.

The jury retired for half an hour, then returned to the court with a query. Was there a charge of assault to be determined? Yes, said the judge, in relation to who hit the keeper Butler.

> *There is no proof that I can see that either Savage or Booth assaulted him except that of Woodhouse, and perhaps you may think there should be a verdict in their favour on that count.*

With this endorsement of the community prejudices and perceptions ringing in their ears, the jury retired for another 50 minutes and returned a verdict against both prisoners of 'guilty for night poaching, armed, and not guilty of the assault'.[2]

This time, at least, the jury had followed his clear direction now that it agreed with local sentiment. But the judge was still unhappy with the disregard of his instructions to the jury in the first trial.

On Thursday Mr Shee delivered his sentence. This was his opportunity to further berate all involved for ignoring his previous injunctions to the jury. Referring to the affray at Silver Wood he said that

> *the whole neighbourhood said it was murder; you even talked of it yourselves as a murder; the instinct and feeling of the whole neighbourhood declared it to be a murder. All the facts of the case were distinctly proved, and we had the melancholy spectacle – melancholy as regards the administration*

of justice – after all the facts were proved, of seeing one of the murderers clap his hands in the dock, because what all the people in his neighbourhood declared to be a murder, had been declared in this Court to be only a manslaughter.

Booth, whose actions on the night and subsequently the judge also viewed with considerable distaste, was sentenced to seven years penal servitude. Ginger Savage, 'acting under the influence of that good-for-nothing man', Woodhouse, received only five years.[3]

Mr Shee's outburst perfectly reflected the class divide of the time and place. While the middle classes – of whom Woodhouse should have been a staunch member – saw the event as a straightforward murder, the local working-class community had a much more ambivalent view. That view was tempered by centuries of conflict over the game laws, the appropriation of the commons and the increasingly obvious gap between those who had and those who had not, opened up by the furnaces of the Industrial Revolution.

While the various legal proceedings were being conducted, the country all around was riven with class antagonisms. The newspapers carried a perpetual litany of strikes, lockouts, demonstrations and other forms of social and industrial action. On 9 January there had been a stormy reform meeting at Derby where 'The friends of Parliamentary reform mustered in strong force'.[4] Another large meeting took place at Leeds on 29 January. In October the home of a saw grinder in Sheffield was bombed by trade unionists because he was considered to be treating his workers unfairly. This was one of many attacks that were part of the ferment of union activity in this area[5] and which became known as 'the Sheffield Outrages'.[6] Sheffield was chosen as the location of a national trades union conference in July, 1866. These and similar disruptions around the country sparked, in 1867, a Royal Commission on the Trade Unions.

Also at the local level, yet reflecting national matters, were black-edged newspaper editions mourning the death of the prime minister, Lord Palmerston, and an ongoing panic at the Fenian outrages. These brought about a boosting of police numbers in the area.[7] Local controversies continued over the supply of water to Sheffield and the poor quality of the smoky air. So did protestations about the game laws and their savage consequences. Writing to the editor of the *Sheffield Daily Telegraph* in early May 1867, a correspondent only willing to call him or herself 'Treble X' expressed a widely-held view:

> *Sir,*
>
> *I see another case of alleged game trespass in your paper of Wednesday; and in that case the gamekeeper brutally assaulted a poor man who was said to be doing no further harm than gathering herbs ... I am weary of seeing every week reports of charges made against poachers and trespassers in pursuit of game. I say it would be better that not a single hare or pheasant, not a rabbit or head of grouse should be left alive in the land rather than that men should be tempted into poaching in this way.*

The letter writer went on to reveal the hidden costs of maintaining the game laws and the privileges of those who benefited by them:

Why should ratepayers be called upon to protect the Duke of Omnium's or Mr Anybody's game? Practically, it comes to that, for the country has to support the innumerable prisoners who are sent to gaol in game cases, and the parishes have to support their families. Sir, I have great respect for the rights of property, but surely no man has the right to maintain for his amusement a property which becomes a public injury and a public nuisance. This is the centre of a game-preserving district, and not a week passes without producing its crop of offences against the game-laws. I wonder our local agitators don't take up this matter and bring it under the notice of our members.

I remain, yours, &c.[8]

As Treble X noted, the papers were full of 'desperate affray' accounts of violent clashes between poachers and game keepers.[9] These events continued long after the fates of William and Myra Sykes were settled by the courts,[10] though one such affray was to play a part in their sundered lives.

6

Dear Husband ...

you must not delay riteing if you
can it will ease my mind

Myra Sykes to William Sykes, 15 March 1867

William Sykes, narrowly convicted of manslaughter, was
sent back to West Riding Prison in Wakefield. He had
been imprisoned there with the other poachers while
awaiting trial at Leeds. As number 8740 he would now
idle away his time in solitary confinement, awaiting
arrangements to transport him to far distant Swan River.

Wakefield is relatively close to Rotherham, so Myra
was able to visit William during this period though it
is not clear that she did. But she certainly wrote to him.
In the original bundle of letters discovered at Toodyay
there is an envelope from Rotherham, postmarked
9 September 1866. The letter and envelope are now long
gone from the archives,[1] but it confirms that Myra and
William were in at least some contact with each other.
Travel was difficult and expensive. There were serious
industrial disputes, cattle plagues, Fenian scares and
cholera outbreaks throughout the region at this time,[2]
further unsettling the country and adding to the possible
hazards of even a relatively short journey.

Soon after Myra posted her letter, William was
transferred from Wakefield to Portsmouth Prison where
he would await transportation to the Swan River in
Western Australia. Conditions at Portsmouth were
probably preferable to those of Wakefield. Portsmouth

was a much larger establishment, used almost solely as a holding house for those awaiting transportation. The cells were iron boxes 6 feet high and 7 feet by 4 feet, with dark corrugated iron walls. Most had only the light from a small window in the door and seem to have been without heating or ventilation. These conditions encouraged ill health in many prisoners, as Surgeon Saunders from the convict transport ship *Norwood* would shortly discover during the course of his duties.

According to a former inhabitant of Portsmouth Prison, writing in 1866, the prison routine was oppressive and exhausting. Morning cell cleaning was completed in darkness, with few facilities and in a great rush. The morning cup of cocoa, gulped down, was followed immediately by chapel and then a few minutes break. Then there was a rush for the few toilets – 'the grand scramble', he called it. After this the convicts went to work doing heavy manual labour in the docks – lifting, carrying, cleaning. The work was hard and dangerous; many were injured. In these respects prison experience reflected the hardships and risks of industrial labour; inmates may have noticed little difference between occupational work and gaol work, or the disciplines of either. As far as we know, William escaped any serious physical injury, though he must have been emotionally wounded, no matter how well he hid it.[3] So, having survived a sojourn in Portsmouth Prison, William was next to board a sailing ship for transportation to Western Australia.

The extreme severity of the British legal system during the eighteenth century had caused the country's prisons to overflow. When the American Revolution succeeded in 1783 the British were deprived of a colonial dumping ground for their convicts. The overcrowding of prisons and hulks, combined with the strategic necessity of establishing a military presence and settlement in the antipodes, led to the decision to establish a penal colony at Botany Bay, part of present-day Sydney.

The First Fleet sailed in late 1787, celebrating Christmas at sea and making landfall in January 1788. Almost 1500 male and female convicts, military personnel, guards (some with families), accompanied by assorted naval folk and administrators founded modern Australia as a gaol. Conditions for convicts aboard the First Fleet were relatively pleasant as some care had been taken to provision and resource the fleet for its epic journey, in some ways equivalent to a modern voyage to the moon. But many subsequent convict voyages became notorious for their cruelty, inhumanity and depravity. And life was little better for the survivors when they arrived in New South Wales. For the first years of the colony, crime, corruption and abuses of all kinds were the normal fare of everyday life and a convict's lot was often not a happy one, as many of their surviving accounts testify.[4]

Eventually, the excesses of the system led to government inquiries, as a result of which conditions were improved to some extent, though it became clear by the 1840s that the transportation of convicts to New South Wales would have to cease. The growing numbers of free settlers were concerned by transportation and had higher aspirations for their colony than its status as a vast penal institution. In the early 1850s transportation to the east coast of Australia officially ended.

By the time William was delivered to the Swan River, the darkest days of transportation were far in the past.

The barbarism of Norfolk Island and Port Arthur in Van Diemen's Land survived only in the more painful memories of a diminishing few former convicts and gaolers. But the continuing need to ease the pressure on British gaols, combined with the economic problems of the Swan River Colony, resulted in the introduction of transportation to Western Australia. From 1850[5] convicts – male only – had been despatched to the Swan in an effort to kill two birds with the one stone. And while the transportation trade was now a regulated and relatively trouble-free business, the lengthy sea voyage and the lot of the luckless transports once landed were difficult, as William would soon discover for himself.

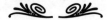

Myra Sykes now speaks directly to her 'dear husband' for the first time in this story. On 15 March 1867 she writes to William, labouring in Portsmouth Prison. She introduces the despondencies and worries that will concern her through all the long years of erratic correspondence with William:

> *Dear husband i rite these few line to you hopeing to find you better than it leavs us at present ...*

Myra, not for the first and far from the last time, broaches her bewilderment at William's tardiness in writing. Bone's wife had received two letters from her husband, who accompanied William on the long voyage to oblivion:

> *i have been very uneasy sinse you did not rite my childen cried When we got no letter Mrs Bone has*

*got two leters sinse i got one will you please to rite
to me and send me wird how you are getting on i
have bilt myself up thinking i shall get to you some
time or another ...*

There is news of Myra's mother, who has not been
well, and of the Judas, Woodhouse, who Myra hears

*has been for giving himself up severl times when
he has been in drink i hope he will.*

He never did.

Myra and the children are missing William sorely:

*we have wished scores of time you was comeing
in to the house we should syuse [squeeze] you to
deth ...*

Kindly, William's brother Joshua has invited Myra to
his family home. No such invitation seems to have been
extended from other members of William's family:

*Joshua Sykes has sent word for me to go to their
house but i have not had time to go*

Again, Myra beseeches William to write:

*you must not delay riteing if you can it will ease
my mind if you can ...*

Then,

*if it ever lays in your power to send for us when
you get abroad i would freely sell all up to come
to you if i possibly could ...*

Finally, the children send their love to their vanished
father:

Dear farther do pleas to writ to is i Sends one 100
kiss for you thirza Sykes …
a kiss will xxxxx
Ann Sykes sends Dear xxxxx
father i send a 100 kiss for you
Alfred sens kiss kinds
Love to you

News of William's impending departure to Australia
must have broken about the time Myra wrote this letter.
It crossed one, now lost, from William. In his letter,
which was sent via Charles Hargreaves and sister
Elizabeth at Park Gate, William gave vent to a rare
expression of emotion, calling his children 'the strings of
my heart'.

Myra wrote straight back to William upon receiving
the news, only four days after her previous
correspondence. By the spelling and general expression,
this letter seems to have been written on Myra's behalf,
probably by Charles Hargreaves again, perhaps by
another man's hand. Despite this, Myra's distress comes
through clearly. She wants to travel to Portsmouth to see
William but cannot afford the expensive journey:

*I do not see how I could possibly undertake the
journey this week, being without money*

Myra needed all the money she had to pay the rent.
But she still held out the hope that she may yet manage
the trip, despite her various difficulties:

*I will come if I come alone for none of them say
anything about coming them-selves, or assisting
me to do so either*

Later in the letter, after sympathising with William's incarceration while the betrayer Woodhouse walks free,[6] Myra returns to the deep tensions between the families and, perhaps, to another matter that has come between her and her husband:

> *I feel greatly hurt that you should send your letters to you Brothers & Sisters before me – for although we are separated there is no one I value and regard equal to you – and I should like you to still have the same feeling towards me*

Myra then repeats a constant theme of her early correspondence, a hope that would burn throughout the long, dark years of separation:

> *if there is ever a chance of our being permitted to join you again even though it be in a far off land, both the children and myself will most gladly do so*

Then Myra asks if, like Bone, his co-convicted, William wishes to have pictures of the children made to take with him into exile.

> *Will you let me know?*

It seems that he never did.

Myra finishes with sentiments that would become the perpetual conclusions of her small, scribbled notes to William:

> *I cannot give you up. I live in the hope of our being together again somewhere before we end our days*

At around the same time, possibly accompanying Myra's letter, William was also honoured with a letter from Charles Hargreaves. Married to William's sister, Elizabeth, in 1845, Hargreaves was originally a blacksmith at Wingfield St, Greasbrough, but now lived in Park Gate, a well-to-do section of Rotherham. Hargreaves, probably a Unitarian, was clearly not prepared to advance Myra the money she needed to visit William in Portsmouth Prison. But he was not stinting with moral advice. He penned a wordy and severe homily to William, reminding him of his sins and the need for redemption:

> *William, my advice to you is that you obey all that are in authority over you and Let your conduct be good and try to gain that which you have lost i mean your character. Let me beg of you to pray to our heavenly father and his son Jesus Christ to give you a clean heart and right spirit within and then all your troubles and anxieties of this world will be small when compared with the Joy and happyness of that bright world above ...*

With all the earnestness and sternness of a lay preacher, Hargreaves continued for another few paragraphs in like vein, with well-meaning advice regarding the proper state of William's soul and urging him to seek

> *the salvation of the Gospel, which reveals God to us which makes us acquainted with his nature, his attributes his character, his government and which especially unfolds to us that scheme of mercy in which he had most clearly manifested his glory ...*

Hargreaves then chooses to remind William Sykes of a section of the Gospel that could hardly have been of comfort to a man about to be split asunder from home, country and family for the rest of his life:

William ... when they was leading Jesus to the cross and there followed a great company of people which also bewailed and lamented him but Jesus turning unto them said Daughters of Jerusalem weep not for me but for yourselves

Seizing on a remark in William's previous letter, which Myra had obviously shared with him, Hargreaves then seeks to generate some emotional capital from his knowledge of William's love for his children:

i believe you said your children was the strings of your heart now i say let Christ be the strings of your heart

He concludes this earnest epistle – written on a page of cash-book paper – with some family news that once again demonstrates the divisions between Myra and William's relations:

Dear William your brother John would give your little boy a good school education but your Dear Wife cannot find time to send him to school

And with that sting in the tail, Charles Hargreaves of the lower case personal pronoun blessed William:

i conclude with the blessing of God almighty the father son and the holy ghost may remain with you both now and forever amen

Reading between these lines it seems likely that William's family had decided it would be best for everyone if they all made a clean break. This may explain their reluctance to visit him in Portsmouth. 'You have to be cruel to be kind', as at least one or two of the relations would have undoubtedly recalled. There is also a strong suggestion that William's older brother, John, and perhaps one or more of his other siblings, had done quite well in life and were perhaps not prepared to be seen visiting relatives in goal.

Not surprisingly, Myra did not see things this way and resented what she interpreted as their cold-heartedness, no doubt reinforced by William's habit of sending letters to her through his family. The relationship between Myra and William's family would be a continuing and uncomfortable subtext through their long and difficult correspondence.

William Sykes also seems to have had at least a degree of respect for Hargreaves. Instead of putting Myra as next of kin in the Portsmouth Prison register, he named Charles Hargreaves. Whether this was an attempt to sever his ties with Myra and assert those of his family is impossible to know, but what is known is that he did make other efforts to erase documentary traces of Myra. When he arrived at Fremantle Prison after a long voyage he would claim that he had no wife at all.

Myra's next surviving letter to William was written on 8 April 1867. In it she fusses over the various articles of food, clothing and other necessities she has painstakingly and at considerable expense gathered together for his long journey. She also repeats her plaintive reminder:

If you have the chance to earn any mone in Australia you must save it all up and i will do the same, that if there is a chance of our rejoining you we may be able to do so.

Myra's simple hope for reunion was not as forlorn as it might seem. Upon successfully petitioning the Colonial Office it was now possible for wives and children to obtain an assisted, perhaps even a free passage, from England to the Swan in order to rejoin their husbands. Whether Myra was aware of this, we cannot say. It seems unlikely that she was, judging by the tone of this and her other letters and her misinformation about tickets of leave given in her evidence at the second trial. Although the relevant Colonial Office files for the most likely period of petitioning are available and include a number of successful requests from wives of convicts to be reunited in Western Australia, there is no official record of such an approach from Myra or of anyone on her behalf.[7] But the hope of being once again together with William never left her. Nor did it leave at least one of Myra and William's children through the long years of growing up without a father.

William and Myra Sykes were now at the beginning of a new reality in their lives. The long years of separation, tears and intermittent communication commenced with William's farewell to England on a sea voyage that would deposit him and more than 250 other transports on the harsh shores of Western Australia's Swan River.

7 Aboard the Norwood

We desire to elevate the moral sentiments, and arouse the
intellectual faculties of those amongst whom we circulate.

William Irwin, Religious Instructor, in *Norwoodiana, or Sayings and Doings On*
Route to Western Australia, Number 1, week ending 27 April 1867

Dr Saunders, Staff Surgeon, Royal Navy was a firm but fair man. He signed aboard as Surgeon Superintendent, victualler and general overseer of the government's interests on a hired ship, the 13-year-old *Norwood*, early in March 1867. The surgeon's duties upon the 785 ton, Sunderland-built vessel captained by Master Frank Bristow were varied. As well as the health of the crew, convicts, guards, passengers and their families, he was charged with supplying food and drink and with disciplining any infractions of the regulations, of which there were many.

Saunders's log[1] of the voyage that transported 254 convicts – among them William Sykes, Bone, Bentcliffe and Teale – to the far ends of the earth began with a comprehensive set of rules for prisoners. Quietness and orderliness were virtues; improper language and talking to crew or guards were vices. Other directives covered responsibilities for cleanliness, fairness of mess provisioning, airing of bedding and general behaviour. This initial list of rules ended: 'The Men are cautioned, that a faithful account of all their good and bad qualities will be rendered to the Governor of the Colony on landing, foundered [*sic*] entirely on their behaviour on board ship.'

Then Saunders continued with 27 punishable offences, ranging from 'want of cleanliness of prison or mess' to 'giving false alarm of fire'. In between came warnings against 'standing up on bulwarks or going aloft without my permission', making false accusations, spreading discontent about rations, using threatening language and smoking tobacco.

A number of convicts and their guards were to be the object of Saunders's displeasure, which usually meant spending time in leg irons in 'the Box', usually for up to a month after their release from solitary confinement, or at least as solitary as it was possible to be on a small sailing ship packed with over 300 people. Despite these severe punishments, Saunders was not above admitting any mistakes he made. In the case of one convict, ironed and confined for stealing food, the surgeon was reliably informed by a number of other convicts and guards that the man was innocent. Saunders had him released from the Box, though kept him in leg irons for the full month of the original punishment.

Having efficiently – on paper at least – regulated the transportees, Saunders proceeded to do the same for their guards, who were to rise at 6 am (their wives half an hour later), breakfast at 7.30 and carry out their various duties and chores until 9 pm. By this time, 'their wives and children must be in bed for the night and one light only to be kept in the barracks'. Sometimes, if not more frequently, the gaolers must have wondered if they were not as much prisoners as those they watched over. Certainly the number of charges of insolence and threatening behaviour against a number of them suggests that they were far from a happy company of men.

Then there was the daily routine Saunders devised for the whole of the more than 370 souls at his command – 254 convicts, the guard of 30, their 30 wives and 18 children, four warders on their way to duties at Fremantle's grim limestone gaol, two cabin passengers and the religious instructor, Mr Irwin. The three cooks were to be allowed on deck at 5.15 am. Everyone else was to be up at 5.30 or 'as soon as daylight'. At 6 am they were to begin washing themselves. Such were the numbers involved that this had to be done in divisions, just as with everything else, from eating to exercising. After 8 o'clock breakfast Saunders inspected the sick and had the prison deck cleaned, which was inspected at 9.30; prayers followed. The children went to school in the morning, breaking at 11.30, at which time lime juice was issued all around. 'Dinner' was at noon, followed by an issue of wine and a return to school for the youngsters. At 3.45 the messmen were to muster on deck to receive their group's allotment of salt meat for the following day. Supper was at 5, followed in half an hour by preparations for the night's sleep. There were more prayers at 8, then rounds and, presumably, lights out at 9. Wednesday and Thursday were washing mornings. School was out on Saturday, though library books were exchanged. All men were expected to shave on Tuesdays and Saturdays. Saunders even supervised the effective padlocking of the few water closets, a cause of considerable friction aboard the ship as diarrhoea was a constant complaint of passengers, guards and convicts.

This draconian regime was designed to be fair and to allow all concerned to withstand the hazardous three-month voyage to the Swan River Colony. It was already well established by 2 April 1867, when William Sykes and over 50 other convicts were shipped aboard the *Norwood* from Portsmouth Prison. As well as quickly being acquainted with Surgeon Saunders's carefully devised rules and regulations, the Portsmouth group found that there were already many transports aboard. Some, including John Teale and Henry Bone, had been picked up at Chatham on 28 March. From Portsmouth the *Norwood* proceeded to Portland, where she picked up further human cargo of unwilling emigrants, including the fourth of the transported poachers, John Bentcliffe.

It is likely that the conditions aboard ship were preferable to those in gaol ashore. Before Saunders would accept convicts aboard he visited their shoreside prisons to ascertain their state of health. His descriptions of Portsmouth refer to problems with diarrhoea and respiratory infections, probably the result of damp, draughts and poor diet. When the convicts were transferred aboard ship, they were at least assured of a regular medical inspection and a reasonable, if monotonous, diet. Saunders's log faithfully, even fussily, records the allowances of wine, lime and lemon juice, port, meat and arrowroot (to aid digestion) regularly doled out to prisoners and guards. Before leaving England he was supplied with poor quality meat by the contractor. He complained and even refused to accept at least one large delivery, returning it with a sharp note of complaint.

Just as Saunders was not willing to be put upon by government contractors, nor was he going to brook any infractions of his numerous rules. On 12 April, at 9.30 pm, past the time set down for slumber, he recorded in his log:

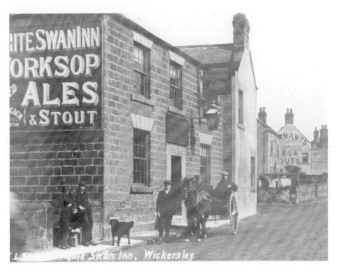

The White Swan Inn, Wickersley, with the Masons' Arms further along
Bawtry Road. Photographed by E L Scrivens, Doncaster, c. 1900-1910.
(Rotherham Metropolitan Borough Council, Archives and Local Studies)

College Square, Rotherham, with the Court House in the background,
c. 1903-1910.
(Rotherham Metropolitan Borough Council, Archives and Local Studies)

564A

1867 March 15

Dear Husband i rite these
few lines to you hopeing
to find you better than it
leaves us at present i have
been very uneasy since you did
not rite my hildren cried
wehen we got no leter MosBon
has got troo leters since i got
one will you please to rite to
me and send me word how
you are getting on i have bee
myself up thinking i shall get

First page of Myra's letter to William, March 15, 1867.

506A

List of articles enclosed
in the box.
Three Spice loaves - 3 lbs Cheese
One Pork pie — 1 Mince pie
2 lbs Sugar — 2 by Tea — 2 do
Bottle of Tobacco - Parcel of Tobacco
Packet of Spice - Quire of Paper
4 Books — ½ Doz. Pipes
Old favourite Tobacco Pouch
Thread needles Buttons &c.
Alfred sends his little pocket
knife.
Three Bottles of ink & pens
2 Fig cakes— Apples oranges
and Lemons—
Bottle of pickles 1½ lb Bacon

Myra's list of articles assembled for William Sykes to take into penal servitude. (Battye Library, WA)

The sailing ship *Norwood*. (National Maritime Museum, UK)

William Sykes' shipboard journal aboard the *Norwood*.
(Battye Librbary, WA)

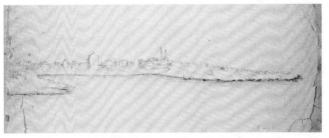

Fremantle in 1868, looking south across Arthur Head.
(By George Walpole Leake, Battye Library, WA)

Fremantle Prison, showing the warders' housing in the foreground,
around 1855. (By W. Pearce Clifton, Battye Library, WA)

The Toodyay Convict Depot before its demolition in 1934.
(Photograph by Stuart Gore, Battye Library, WA)

564A

October 20th
1875

Dear father I write these few lines
hopeing to find you better than it
leaves us at presant my mother as
been very ill and me my self
and I am a bit better Dear father
we think you have quite forgot us all
my sister Ann takes it hard at
you not writing oftener I must
tell you that sister Ann as to nice
boys the oldest is a fine little
fellow well I must tell you what
a stout young man my brother
Alfred as got and Thirza is a
stout young womman poor Ann
is very thin Ann usband and
Alfred works at aldwarke

Letter of William Sykes the younger to his father in the Swan River
colony, 1875. (Battye Library, WA)

Dear Husban I hand you
to my hart it had my
Ann I have had her
Both times of her
confindments and
by this gating on
gain

I shall sends our
nearist and dearted
Love to you
with X 1000 kiss
Dear Husband you
must excuse writing

Myra's letter to William, possibly
the last she ever wrote him.
Probably 1876. (Battye Library, WA)

Supposed site of William Sykes'
grave, Toodyay Cemetery.

Silver Wood as it is.

St Mary's Church, Greasborough.

Restored Newcaste (Toodyay) Gaol.

Cells in the restored Newcastle (Toodyay) Gaol.

Appoximate location of William and Myra Sykes' home in Midland Road, Masborough. The Woodman pub in the background.

Slight disturbance in Prison, singing and fife playing – Accompanied by Mr Irwin and Warders, entered the Prison and addressed a few words to them with reference to their conduct, after which all again became quiet.

Brisk, firm and efficient was the way Dr Saunders went about his work. His government paymasters were well served by his approach to his duties, as were those in his charge. On the evidence of his log, the doctor was a conscientious and, on the evidence of the voyage itself, an effective carer. Apart from prescribing arrowroot, though, there was little he could do about the first problem that was to plague William Sykes and his companions.

The *Norwood* heaved up her anchor early on the evening of 18 April. By 5.30 she was under sail, bound for warmer but harder climes. All aboard were granted extra time above decks, 'permitting a long last lingering look at the rugged coast of Old England', as Mr Irwin would later record. That night, many of the convicts, the guards and their families were introduced to the delights of a nineteenth century sea voyage. Almost everyone was seasick. Saunders noted this in his professional manner. In his tersely-worded diary, William Sykes simply scrawled:

*Sailed from Portland the 18
head wind ruff night*

It was to be the first of many such nights and days. Saunders frequently writes of the disabled condition of the non-sailors aboard due to seasickness caused by inclement weather. Occasionally, the ship seems to have been rolling so much – 'very strong sea rowling', as William described one such occasion – that the handwriting in Saunders's log becomes illegible. He went through considerable quantities of arrowroot during the voyage.

While the convicts were allowed a small number of personal items, most of them would not have had anything to help them with seasickness. William's own kit consisted of the box of 'Articals' Myra had sent him, together with a few items of clothing:

flanel Shirt 1
Belts 2
flanel compforter
1 anchifes pocket
2 caps
2 purs
1 comb
2 Cotton shirts and Looking glass 1
4 needles and thread
6 anks

He had also received from Myra while in gaol at Portsmouth a box of food and personal items. In it were

Three Spice loaves – 2 lbs Cheese
One Pork pie – one mince pie
2lbs sugar – 2 tea 2 do.
Packet of Spice – quire of paper
4 books – ½ doz pidoz pipes
Bottle of Tobacco – parcel of Tobacco
Old favourite Tobacco pouch
Thread needles Buttons &c
Three bottles of ink & pens
2 Fig cakes – Apples oranges and lemons
Bottle of pickels 1¼ lbs Bacon
Alfred sends his little pocket knife

Most of the food was long gone by now and would not have been of much interest to a seasick man in any case. After a day or two of *mal de mer*, William might have looked at his gaunt and strained features in the looking glass. But the shirts, handkerchiefs, purses, comb, sewing gear and scarf would not have been of much use at that time. No doubt he would find good work for them when he finally did reach Western Australia. In the meantime the tobacco pouch and pipe would have been his only comfort.

Myra had done her best with the meagre resources available to her. Accompanying the box she had written:

> *I have sent you all that I possibly could and am only sory that it is not in my power to send you more.*

She had received a letter from William.[2] After reading it Myra visited William's sister, Elizabeth. She donated 'two of the smallest spice loaves' to the cause of William's diet and also gave Myra a shilling towards the cost of sending the loaves. Myra then went to William's other sister, Rebecca, with the letter but 'she could not do anything towards it'.

This must have angered Myra, though she almost manages to hide her hurt, going on to tell William that she had also visited Emma who had 'sent the other spice loaf and mince pie'. Mindful of William's soul, and no doubt prompted by her pious husband, Elizabeth had also sent a bible and a religious pamphlet. Elder brother John donated two books. A friend, it seems, had contributed an ounce of tobacco and Myra had also walked to Sheffield in hope of finding a clasp knife to send. Unable to do so, young Alfred had presumably donated his 'little pocket knife' to whatever might have been his father's greater need.

As well as the expenses involved in obtaining these items, the postage costs from Sheffield to Portsmouth were severe. She writes:

If Saturday had been pay day I might perhaps have been able to get a trifle more for you.

Already she was finding it hard to make ends meet. Myra had paid 4/6 for transport of the box to Bristol and John was going to pick up the cost of mail from there to William in Portsmouth Prison. Altogether an expensive undertaking, especially so for a family that had lost its chief breadwinner and was now to be at least partly dependent on the charity of relations, some of whom were clearly not Myra's friends. Although Myra was in work, she also had the task of managing the children and coordinating communication with her 'Dear husband', now torn away from home, family and country and transported across rough seas to a very different place.

While Surgeon Saunders had the responsibility for the health, food and discipline of the gaolers and the gaoled aboard the *Norwood*, Mr William Irwin had the care of their education, their morals and their souls. Irwin was an experienced convict ship voyager, this being his sixth passage as a religious officer. He wasted no time in establishing the means by which he would take care of the religious, moral and even the intellectual lives of his charges. The main instrument of his office was the ship's weekly journal, titled *Norwoodiana*.[3] The first issue, for the week ending 27 April 1867, stated, using the royal plural that 'We desire to elevate the moral sentiments, and arouse the intellectual faculties of those amongst whom we circulate'.

This inaugural edition of *Norwoodiana* established the basic structure of the following 10, plus one supplement, that would appear remorselessly each week of the long voyage out. There was an introductory article, usually on some improving topic, by Irwin himself, followed by information about Western Australia, the ship's progress during the week, snippets of news and announcements of the social and entertainment events. Sometimes there were poems and later various pseudonymous contributions, notably 'Adventures in India' by 'An Old Soldier' that appeared at some length from Issue 4 until the end of the voyage. Many of the issues even aspired to pictorial dimensions, with better or worse drawings of Gage Roads, Fremantle, Aborigines and, as the ship neared its destination, an emu.

As with the more practical responsibilities and methods of Dr Saunders, Religious Instructor Irwin also had his regime to superimpose upon that laid down by the surgeon. There were bible readings, a choir, poetry readings (Wordsworth) and amateur dramatics (Hood and even Shakespeare). News of these frequent events was spiced up with various articles by Irwin on charity, home, self-respect and other such moralising topics, all aimed at providing the convicted with firm guidelines on their future careers in the Swan River and, if they were lucky and industrious enough, afterwards.

The pages of Irwin's periodical reveal a pompous but right-minded man who took the safekeeping of souls very seriously indeed. Even the entertainments provided for the passengers and – if only incidentally – for the convicts were described in a mixture of serious prose and what may have passed at the period for lively wit. Describing an amateur performance, presumably by the passengers, held on 7 June, Irwin writes:

> *On Friday afternoon of the 7th inst; a novelty was produced in the shape of a 'Nigger Entertainment (a la Christy's Minstrels)' on the upper deck. The performers appeared in appropriate 'Nigger' attire, their visages and hands having undergone the operation of 'Corking'.*
>
> *Several songs were sung with the accompaniments (ordinarily imagined to be indissolubly connected with Ethiopian Serenaders) of Bones, tamborine, banjo, Pipe and Concertina – and some dances of a very energetic and* sole *inspiring character were performed. The entertainment was enlivened by some excellent conundrums and witticisms, and everything considering there had been little or no rehearsal passed off remarkably well.*

While the witticisms and conundrums may not have been the usual entertainment of William Sykes and his fellow transports, William certainly witnessed this performance and even thought it worthy of mention in his sparse journal.

7 niggers friday night

What William and the other convicts made of this uplifting activity, often couched in what to most of them would have been obscure phrases such as 'rude Boreas' and 'piscatorial pastimes', is difficult to know. Presumably, like William, they related well to the blackface minstrel show, long a popular form of entertainment. But there is little evidence that any of them contributed to the pages of *Norwoodiana*. We hear only about a small selection of their activities and attitudes through the eyes and the words of Irwin himself. Probably most were either totally unimpressed. Some would have been scornful of Irwin's well-meant but sanctimonious efforts, which included such exhortations as

> *Attention is particularly directed to the careless manner in which many of the hammocks are slung for the night. The lashings should be carefully examined and tested every time the hammock is slung. Several lately have given way & some narrow escapes of serious consequences experienced.*

Despite these almost inevitable characteristics in someone of Irwin's time, place and station, there are hints that he harboured some progressive, even faintly radical, views. In one article on the freedom of the press, Irwin passionately declared the rights of what would now be called the fourth estate: 'We owe no allegiance to those in power beyond the respect and esteem they seem anxious to deserve and our columns are open to all without favour of affection ... The only censor we acknowledge is Common Sense – the only influence we bend to, is good taste.'

Irwin also had strong views on the damaging nature of the game laws, an increasingly common stand among the middle classes of the time. William Sykes would have read with considerable interest and perhaps some bitterness the article Irwin wrote in *Norwoodiana* 2, titled 'A Step in the Right Direction':

We beg to inform our Norwoodian readers that the restrictions which have hitherto existed upon our constitutional rights and liberties are now to a certain extent removed inasmuch as, that worst of all offences (to the landed proprietor) is, or may now be, considered at an end, and the almost capital crime of poaching done away with. This modification of the Game Laws (laws under the injustice of which the people of England have suffered so long) ...

But despite these evidences of progressive attitudes, Irwin shared the prevailing views of his contemporaries with regard to the indigenous occupiers of the land to which the *Norwood* was bound. In response to queries about the existence or otherwise of Aborigines in Western Australia, Irwin hastened to assure them, in accordance with the prejudice of the period, that

the 'blackfellow' is still very numerous and not likely to become extinct for a length of time, if, what appears to be a law of nature – the savage in course of time succumb to their whiter but more civilized brother and the vices and evil habits which he adopts so much more readily, than any good white man may try to teach him.

The religious instructor followed this with what purported to be but was in fact a hopelessly inaccurate short vocabulary of the local language.[4] If the new arrivals were to have any conversation with the native Mooro, Beeloo and Beeliar people of the Perth region, they would have to conduct it in pidgin English or sign language. But the voyagers, their ignorance barely lit by

Irwin's well-intentioned attempt at education, were not to know this.

Between them, Surgeon Saunders and Religious Instructor Irwin erected an efficient regulation of time, space, attitude and behaviour for those in their charge. What they did, when, how and where they did it were all controlled by an elaborate network of rules designed to make each convict continually aware that he was a number rather than a name. It was the perfect preparation for those who were on their way to years, decades and lifetimes of administrative and judicial direction of their every waking – and even sleeping – hour.

8 *A Weight of Woe*

the outlandic Ocan the tropic
the medary island the cannary
Island the peak of tinereff
along the coast of affrecca
and other peak mountains

From the diary of William Sykes aboard the *Norwood*, May 1867

With all these carefully prepared constraints upon her cargo the *Norwood* ploughed on towards the extremities of the earth. William Sykes recorded some of the highlights. From their vantage point at the other end of the ship's hierarchy, Saunders and Irwin dutifully filled in log books. Together they tell the story of this voyage to incarceration, misery and desolation.

After the first few days and nights of rolling swells and seasickness, the company aboard was quickly settled into the prescribed routines. Such clockwork regulation, combined with the inevitable monotony of day after day of empty sea and sky, soon took its toll. Saunders reports the first trouble within two weeks. Not a convict but one of their guards was insubordinate. This established a pattern of insubordination, pilfering and threatening language that was shared by both the guards and their charges.

William Sykes does not appear in either Saunders's or Irwin's records. He was either too well behaved or too clever to be caught. Perhaps he took part in Irwin's reading and writing classes. Although he had been taught the basics of literacy at Sunday School and Day

School, William was no scholar. Regardless, he set down those incidents that impressed him for one reason or another. His diary, unlike the surgeon's log, registers Easter, perhaps prompted by the sermonising and moralising of Irwin, who was assiduous in carrying out his responsibilities. The Canary Islands and Tenerife were only glimpsed off the weather beam on 11 and 12 May but William was impressed enough with the sight to accord it a place in his chronicle.

Between Easter and 21 May there is a long silence in William's shipboard journal. He may have been in the same shattered state as most of the passengers and convicts, the result of seasickness. Seasickness sounds like a fairly mild, almost trivial, discomfort but it is a profoundly disturbing and unpleasant experience to which most sufferers would prefer death. True seasickness is depressing and disabling and it takes some time to recover from a serious bout. When William did begin again on the single sheet decorated with a flower impress that we are calling his diary, he laboriously inscribed his first observation:

Caut a shark on the 21st of May

It was a bad omen. The diary goes on to tell us of

a Death the same Day a funeral the 22nd.

James Smith had been ill when he came aboard. Saunders treated him as best he could but it was soon obvious to the doctor that the man was dying. He took his time. Saunders's log records his progressive weakening and 'sinking' each day up to his last, mentioned by William. Irwin dutifully recorded Smith's death at 6 pm on Wednesday, 22 May. Smith was buried hastily at sea, the tropical clime making rapid disposal of the corpse a priority.

The City of Shanghai, a clipper bound for England, hove to the day after Smith's burial and took letters for what had once been home. William may have written to Myra, though he probably did not. He had already proved a fickle and irregular correspondent, as Myra would hint in later letters. Coming across another ship in these well-traversed sea lanes was not as unusual as might be thought, but it is unlikely that many passengers, voluntary or otherwise, would have been prepared with letters ready.

One life is extinguished, another takes its place. On 26 May William noted:

A birth

Saunders recorded it also, with some satisfaction as deliverer of the baby to the wife of one of the guards, Francis Lindsey. William's diary continues:

Crossed the line the same day 26
which was Sunday

Irwin was pleased to be crossing the Equator on God's day, making mention of it in his Sunday service. Whether or not the sailors carried out their rather less reverential ritual of Crossing the Line, a mock initiation of voyagers into the court of King Neptune, a parodic ceremony traditionally enacted at the crossing, no one tells us. In fact, except for suspicions that a couple of sailors stole bottles of 'medical Comfort Wine', we hear almost nothing of the ship's 39 crew members from Sykes, Saunders or Irwin. Although the convicts, their guards and the other passengers were carefully counted in the *Norwood*'s manifest,[1] no one bothered to name or even number the mariners. The convicts and their keepers were, as effectively as possible, segregated from the sailors, their shantying and their customs. We know from other sources, short- and long-haul ditties, that sailors on the Australia run worked their ships with the traditional shanties for hauling ropes: 'Blow the Man Down', 'Reuben Ranzo', 'Heave Away My Johnny' among others. The convicts may even have heard the old favourite 'Goodbye, Fare Ye Well' drifting into their cramped quarters from time to time, an unwelcome reminder of their fates:

> *It's now we are hauling right out of the dock*
> *Good by fare ye well, goodbye fare ye well.*
> *Where the boys and the girls on the pierhead do*
> *   flock.*
> *Hurrah me boys, we're bound to go.*
> *They give three cheers while the tears downward*
> *   flow,*
> *Good by fare ye well, goodbye fare ye well...*[2]

But at least there was an extra tot of wine and special rations for all as a commemoration of what was, as well as the centre of the globe, the halfway point of the three-month voyage.

The telegraphic terseness of William's diary now becomes almost poetic in its notations of the maritime geography traversed by the *Norwood* as she ran down the west coast of Africa:

> *the outlandic Ocan the tropic*
> *the medary island the cannary*
> *Island the peak of tinereff*
> *along the coast of affrecca*

and other peak mountains
8 days brees. Steady wind 2 June
good wind 3 making preparation
for ruff wether

By 4 June, somewhere in the vast ocean between the landmasses of Africa and South America, the *Norwood* was opposite Rio de Janeiro – or 'Eugener', as William rendered the unfamiliar name of Brazil's major port:

4 oppisit Eugener
Brassil out of the tropic 6 fair
wind not much of it ...

Unlike those ships that brought earlier generations of the cast out to New South Wales and Van Diemen's Land, those bound for the Swan River no longer put into Rio and Cape Town for fresh supplies and respite from the sea. Instead, they picked up the Roaring Forties for a fast passage east, across the Indian Ocean to the Western Australian coast, a trick the old Dutch East Indiamen had learnt well in the previous centuries of trading to the Dutch colony of Batavia (now Indonesia). But it was always a dangerous run in those days. It was fatally easy to miscalculate a ship's position. The rugged Western Australian coast is littered with the wrecks of VOC (Dutch East India Company) ships, some carrying treasure and some bequeathing tales of blood-crazed savagery and legends of castaways mingling with the Aborigines, centuries before the gaol at Botany Bay was founded.

The coast remained treacherous in 1867, but improvements in timekeeping and navigation made it much easier and safer for Master Bristow to determine where he and his ship were on the great empty Indian Ocean and to set a course for Gage Roads outside Fremantle.

There were still dangers though. A few days after William recorded the 'fair wind', he wrote in his diary:

8 strong wind boult in the flihg
jib broke out

Saunders also records heavy winds on these days and the fact that the ship sustained some storm damage. After the jib sail was set there was 'good sailing' for some days, according to William, who was also impressed by the many and large seabirds that wheeled above, behind and before the *Norwood* as she cut through the waves towards the speck on the charts that was Fremantle. He wrote:

albertrosses ollegok cape pigen and other Birds ...

his basic spelling just managing to convey the sightings of the mariner's traditional good luck charm, the albatross, as well as Cape Pigeons and oligarchs.[3]

William seems to have had more luck than Saunders in sighting albatross as Saunders had still not had that pleasure by 13 June. But on 17 June he was able to note that the *Norwood* had met the *Roxburgh Castle*, 55 days outward bound to Madras.

On 19 June, with 'wind in faver', it became very cold, with rain, hail and

very strong sea rowling

Dr Saunders noted that a waterspout had been seen only two miles away from the ship on that day. This weather meant more seasickness for Saunders to treat and note in his log. Cases of diarrhoea, ringworm, coughs and colds also kept him busy with the arrowroot and the lemon juice. But he also found time to pen a note about the poor quality of the shoes issued to the convicts, which had by this time mostly fallen apart.

In his diary for that day a possibly barefoot William wrote:

dreams

That is all there is. No details, just the one word. Perhaps his dreams were of home, Myra, the children, friends and relations, the trial, possibly that night in Silver Wood when everything in William Sykes' hitherto ordinary life went terribly wrong.

Immediately after the 'dream' entry, William writes that it was a

very ruff night 20 dull with strong
swell on 21

On that day, amidst the pitching and the vomiting, another woman gave birth. But this time, as Saunders noted in his log, the baby was stillborn. William simply scrawled

Birth died

The death of a new-born infant in those days of high and expected infant mortality and in the midst of bad weather at sea was not an occasion for much comment. Irwin certainly avoided mention of it in *Norwoodiana* and Saunders includes only a sparse record in his journal. Nor was the death recorded in the official reckoning of numbers embarked and disembarked. The child had come into the world and gone out again with barely a flicker of record other than in these humble documents and its parents' hearts. Migrating mothers commonly reported the deaths of newborn babies, infants and even older children as an almost matter-of-fact consequence of such hazardous voyages.[4]

Now the seas were becoming rough enough to seriously discomfort the convicts who, while they were below decks in their prison, were continually wet and cold. Saunders was concerned about health and safety and was only able to hang half the required number of heaters. Rats were plaguing crew and passengers, though there was at least some relief from Irwin's determined sermonising as the weather was too rough to hold divine service on the twenty-third. From William's point of view it was just another

miserable day

The next few days were much the same, with fair winds but squally rains. On 26 June there was a serious accident. Probably as a consequence of the dirty weather and general misery, the covers on the ship's boiler had not been properly secured. It exploded:

ackedent
with the Boiler and too men
scolded

William writes. It was actually three men scalded, as Dr Saunders notes, 'two rather seriously'.

On the twenty-seventh they again met *The City of Shanghai* but there was nothing else to break the monotony of the same rough weather well into July:

sailing very fast
with squall until the 9 and
then calm and dull

William Sykes, puddler, poacher, transportee and soon to be Swan River convict, morosely ended his diary of the *Norwood*'s second and final convict voyage on 9 July 1867. These are not the last words we will hear directly from William Sykes, and we will hear much more of him through Myra's and his own letters, then, intermittently, through the official documents of penal servitude. Four days after William completed his terse testament he would come in sight of the land where he had been sent to serve for the rest of his life.

On 13 July, at 2.30 in the afternoon, the Rottnest Island lighthouse was spotted from the masthead. It was not long before all those aboard the *Norwood* saw their journey's end. A convict who had arrived at the Swan a year or so earlier described the first sight that William and his shipmates had of their new abode:

> *The first you see of the land of your exile is a rather low coast-line, broken by two rocky islands, which rise out of a long, low reef of sand and rock, and assist in forming a moderately safe roadstead. As you round the northernmost of these, and approach the land more closely, you see it to be covered with a wild heathery scrub, out of which rise here and there wild-looking trees, scantily leaved and of no great beauty ...* [5]

After her brisk 86 day voyage[6] the pilot came aboard at 5 pm and brought *Norwood* into the turquoise waters of Gage Roads, just off the settlement of Fremantle. But, as Saunders noted, the heavy winds made it impossible to land and the ship was forced to lay off for some days. This forced delay was probably frustrating for all aboard, though perhaps least of all for the convicts. They were only taking a few days off their sentences, all of which would involve hard labour in the harsh bush of the colony. From the decks of the *Norwood*, even through the windswept spray, they could see the hulking shape of a large limestone building atop the hill behind the town. 'Conspicuous above all', as the 1866 convict described it. The grim caverns of Fremantle Prison – 'the Convict Establishment' – dominated the rambling seaport and proclaimed the seriousness with which the colony and the British government intended to pursue transportation to the Swan River, now that it had been ended to the eastern side of the continent.

William Sykes and those suffering with him must have viewed this sight with apprehension, even fear. Little in any of their lives, legal or criminal, had prepared them for incarceration in unhealthy British gaols, dangerous sea voyages or for life – and, in all probability, death – on one of the last and hardest frontiers. Before they could begin to work out their crimes on that gulag, though, they would first have to pass through a forbidding limestone gateway to be ironed, uniformed and newly-numbered.

On 14 July the wind finally dropped and at 1 pm the convicts were taken by barges from the *Norwood* to the jetty. Within an hour or so of their departure the ever-efficient and matter-of-fact Surgeon Saunders had birthed the baby of a pensioner guard and his wife. By that time the convicts were being marched in line through the streets of Fremantle and up the hill dominated by the bulk of the prison. Here, they were officially inducted into the system that would totally control their lives for the duration of their punishment. To some extent the transportees had been selected according to the skills they possessed. The original arrangement between the colony and the British government had been for the Swan River to receive convicts of good character who could contribute to the development of the enterprise. Although the original good intentions regarding minor offenders had gradually faded away, the convicts aboard the *Norwood* represented a considerable asset to the colonists and their aspirations.

They were a diverse group. Thirty-three had no occupation and can probably be considered professional criminals – thieves, burglars and footpads. Forty-four of the transports described themselves as labourers, while the remaining 170 odd were a handy miscellany of trades and skills that could be put to good use in a struggling frontier settlement. There were a good number of men from the building trades, including seven bricklayers, seven carpenters, six painters, five masons and two wagoners, together with a sprinkling of architects, engineers, surveyors and glaziers. The new arrivals, who also brought other useful skills to the colony, included six butchers, five fitters and turners, five bakers, four blacksmiths, four sawyers, clerks, farmers, accountants, druggists, a silversmith, shepherd, cooper, a variety of metalworkers, an upholsterer and makers of gut, combs, boilers, packing cases, watches and ropes. There was even a maker of fiddle strings. Thirteen of the men were miners.

Their crimes were many and various: housebreaking, picking pockets, burglary and the usual assortment of offences against property. There were rick burners and arsonists, both common forms of rural protest. There were counterfeiters, utterers, embezzlers, sheep stealers, deserters and other military malefactors as well as receivers of stolen goods. Crimes against the person were also well represented. As well as the Silver Wood poachers, there were murderers, rapists, paedophiles and a committer of incest. All began serving their time together within the massive walls of Fremantle's convict establishment.

The *Cornhill Magazine* convict again provides a contemporary depiction of Fremantle Prison:

Your first impression, on finding yourself within the gates, is a mixed one. The courtyard is very quiet – not unlike that of a large deserted country inn, and the inspection you undergo before going to the baths is a quiet affair, conducted without fuss or nonsense and only carried just as far as is necessary. So far so good. But the windows of the great building before you, being of a thick grey glass, impress you most unpleasantly.

The writer then goes on to recount the initiation of convicts into 'the Establishment':

After inspection on entrance you go to the baths, and now is the time to secure any money you may have with you ... From the baths, which are sensibly and conveniently contrived, you pass into a great yard to be shaved and have your hair cut, both of which operations, let me tell you, will be performed most effectually. Every particle of whisker, every hair of your head which can be made to pass through a flat comb, is taken off unsparingly. They cut the hair pretty close in England, but what they leave on there is a 'luxuriant growth' compared with what they leave on in Australia.

The *Cornhill Magazine* convict had, like William Sykes, spent some time in Portsmouth Prison before being transported. He was able to make some comparisons between the two establishments:

In size, the cells here [Fremantle] are little larger than the iron cages at Portsmouth; but they are built of stone, have a good window, are of good height, and are plastered and whitewashed, have a firm table and sufficient conveniences, and are really cheerful, airy little dens.

As well as this bright picture of prison architecture, this writer also compared the disciplinary system of Fremantle most favourably with that of English gaols:

You have, when not at work, full liberty of entry and egress [to and from the cells]. For about ten minutes at breakfast-time, and the same at dinner and tea, you must be in them; but even then the doors are left open. All the rest of the day out of working hours you can go down to the yard or stay in your cell – as you please. The doors are closed only at night.[7]

Relaxed though these regulations were, those spending their time in Fremantle Prison were constantly reminded of their incarceration by the bulky limestone walls that formed the horizons of their days and the muffled solitude of their nights. Into this place and its practices passed William Sykes, the last poacher transported to Australia.[8]

He was described in the official prison record as 5 feet 6½ inches in height, with light brown hair and grey eyes. His face was oval, his complexion light and his appearance healthy, in contrast to Bone and Bentcliffe who were both described as 'middling stout', bearing the evidence of their livelihoods in the 'coal cuts' on each man. John Teale was of average build, of swarthy complexion and with an oval face. William had a cut on his left knee, perhaps a result of the rough barge crossing to the shore.[9] He was 39 years old and he was sentenced to 'Life'. His time had begun.

But for others who had been aboard the *Norwood*, their time was at an end. Dr Saunders noted in his final log entry, with satisfaction and relief, that he was at last a man free from government service. William Irwin no doubt felt much the same. The *Norwood* had landed her cargo, her 'weight of woe' as Irwin had once described the convicts in his weekly paper, and delivered them to their place of punishment and penance. With all evidence of her convict voyage promptly and efficiently dismantled, the *Norwood* set sail back across the vast waters to the far end of the globe, where Myra Sykes and all her children waited anxiously for word of William. It was to be a long wait.

9

Swan River

The Convicts are coming, oho!, oho!
What a curse to the Swan! What a terrible blow!
No – devil a bit – don't fear, my old bricks,
How much we may learn, if they'll teach us their tricks.

Swan River Song, 1849

Long before the founders of the Swan River colony arrived in 1829 the vast western coast of Australia had been the site of extensive human occupation. For at least 40 000 years the people of this land had moved across its beaches and deserts and through its forests. They had hunted its wildlife, gathered its fruits and celebrated their oneness with the land and all its features. In small bands they had enjoyed more than 200 generations of undisturbed existence in one of the world's most remote places.

Their myths told of the ancestors and creator serpents that had made the sky, the earth and all those who walked upon it. Their legends were sung and danced in ceremonial gatherings. As well as the Dreamtime stories, they also spoke sometimes of more recent events, such as the sighting of strange winged vessels that passed north and south along the rugged coast.[1] Although the indigenous inhabitants would not know this for many centuries, these were the sailing ships of English and Dutch buccaneers and traders. Sometimes the strange vessels were blown onto the jagged reefs at the base of many of the cliffs, their passengers and crews drowned, marooned and even murdered by each other.

In June 1629 a Dutch ship, the *Batavia*, was wrecked on the Abrolhos Islands; the survivors became involved in one of the most chillingly bloodstained stories of maritime history. The English buccaneer, adventurer and naturalist William Dampier made landfall near Derby at what is now King Sound in 1688, describing the local inhabitants as 'the miserabalist people in the world'. Despite this unpromising and inaccurate assessment,[2] Dampier returned in 1699.

The Dutch continued to sail along these ill-fated coasts, despite sometimes being wrecked. While searching for signs of these foundered vessels and their valuable cargoes of treasure in 1696, Willem de Vlamingh hove to off what is now Fremantle and explored the region inland around what would later be the city of Perth. De Vlamingh found little in his voyages and eventually sailed away from Western Australia early in 1697. He took with him the inscribed pewter plate left by Dirk Hartog on the island he named after himself in 1616, when he became the first known European to walk on the western shore of the continent. To mark his accidental discovery, Hartog left some high-class graffiti, a pewter plate he had engraved and nailed to a pole on the island, a message to any future comers that he had been there first.

Over the next several decades Dutch ships plied the Western Australian waters unchallenged and unhindered, other than by the rocks and the elements. It was not until 1791 that the navigator George Vancouver named the great harbour of King George Sound, its maritime and military potential being the cause of the later founding of the settlement now called Albany. Vancouver was followed by a navigator of legendary skill and achievements, Mathew Flinders, who in 1801 sailed by King George Sound on his circumnavigation of the continent.

These explorers, entrepreneurs and the mostly undocumented sealers and whalers who fished these waters had tentative, intermittent and frequently violent contact with the indigenous peoples. Some shipwreck survivors were cast away forever in a savage land as alien as a distant planet. The fates of these lost souls are open to speculation, though there are some legends and some medical evidence to suggest that at least one European male interbred with the indigenous peoples.

All of this was largely unknown when Captain James Stirling, a man with family connections in the Indian Ocean trade, established his ambitious real estate venture in 1829. A British military settlement existed briefly at King George Sound from 1826 but this was succeeded by Stirling's enterprise. He had first contrived to be officially despatched to the Swan River early in 1827, when he explored the hinterland, discovered the availability of fresh water, acres of good farming land and, just as importantly, established the existence of a harbour. Stirling's highly favourable and well-argued report to the British government, hastened by British fears of French occupation, eventually won official support for the establishment of a colonial outpost. Stirling was quick to put himself forward as the logical person to command such a venture.

After a good deal of politicking and governmental shilly-shallying, mainly due to fear of the expense involved, Stirling's abilities and his connections ensured that he was given the position, along with substantial grants of land and other concessions, including the title

'Lieutenant-Governor' and independence from the east coast colony of New South Wales. Stirling sailed aboard *Parmelia*, reaching the Swan in June 1829; here he found Captain Charles Fremantle on *Challenger*, the representative of the British government sent to ensure that Stirling's group of settlers was not beaten to the post by the French. The Swan River Colony had been founded.

The first settlers began those heroic feats of pioneering and establishing European settlement that are the foundation myths of modern Australia. Stirling had determined that, unlike the convict colonies of New South Wales and Van Diemen's Land, the Swan River would be a place for solid, dependable English yeomen to farm and prosper. His exertions in Britain on behalf of his colonial dream had generated a good deal of popular enthusiasm for the Swan, so people clamoured to undertake the same arduous voyage that William Sykes and his companions would take 37 years later, if under very different circumstances.

Between August and December 1829, 18 immigrant ships anchored off Fremantle. This was the start of an initial flurry of settlement. Word of a new, free colony in sunny Australia had an appealing resonance to the solid upper working classes and lower middle classes of Britain, keen to better themselves. Sturdy farmers, artisans and God-fearing Wesleyans were among the first settlers. Usually well-resourced with funds, skills and family, these pioneers displayed the determined focus of successful settlers in Australia and elsewhere in the New World. For the most part they felt they had burnt their bridges to wherever they had come from and so must make their new lives a success or suffer the dreaded nineteenth century disgrace of penury. They were inclined not to be dissuaded from their aspirations by climate, landscape, red tape or natives. As a catch-phrase of the time went, they were 'sterling stock'. These hardy settlers were not of the class represented by Henry Jubb and those others who benefited from England's game laws. Such people had no need to emigrate. Nor were many of them of the same class as William Sykes; they were often too poor to leave.

Those who did come, quickly pushed inland, establishing viable settlements at Fremantle, Perth, Bunbury on the coast south of Perth and a few inland spots, including Newcastle (Toodyay). In the long years of his transportation at the Swan River William Sykes would come to know these places well.

There were the inevitable disasters, including the colonists tempted to the Swan by the ambitious immigration and settlement schemes of Thomas Peel, in which settlers were attracted by the promise of land grants. Peel negotiated an enormous grant of one million acres with the British government and various private backers, planning to bring 10 000 emigrants to the colony. Some of his backers got cold feet and, ultimately, only 400 immigrants arrived in 1830, too late to take up grants as the deadline for their arrival had passed. Four hundred were simply forsaken along the coast, many subsequently dying from dysentery, scurvy and the other consequences of heat, rain and hardship.[3] Around the same time another emigrant ship was wrecked nearby, the crew, passengers and even his own wife and children abandoned by the captain. A few were saved by the bravery of a navy officer.

Despite these setbacks, the colony pushed ahead, expanding ever further into the lands that had once been those of the indigenous inhabitants alone. At first, relations with the Aborigines were reasonably cordial, but within a year there was misunderstanding, conflict and violence. The local bands resisted, especially those led by Midgegooro and Yagan, which led to an escalating conflict of raids, retribution, ambush and summary execution, usually performed in a particularly savage manner.

These conflicts culminated in the fateful events of 28 October 1834, in which Stirling led a party of 24 mounted civilians and troops against 80 Murray River people. At least 15 Aboriginal men, women and children were shot dead in what is now called the Pinjarra Massacre. This was followed by systematic harassment of local groups, their rapid dispersal to the edges of settlement and their concentration into easily managed food depots or camps, often proclaimed as Aboriginal reserves.

The establishment of such a depot in 1833 had prompted one early settler, sympathetic to the indigenes, the enigmatic Robert Lyon, to caustically twist this name to its other meaning of a game reserve: 'What does the local Government mean? Does it intend to keep the natives as a game reserve to be fed and shot at leisure?'[4] Even in this far-flung edge of empire the game laws and the social conflicts they engendered, produced strong reverberations of home, which were amplified by the colony's foundation rationale of providing cheap land and access to its resources – at the expense of those who were already there.

But Lyon was a solitary voice among the settlers. The massacre at Pinjarra, one of many such that took place around the continent, effectively ended Aboriginal resistance to European occupation and the settlement of the Swan River was able to proceed in relative peace, if uncertain prosperity.

After some initial progress, the Swan River Colony faltered, a victim in many ways of its own success. Those who did brave the long sea voyage and the perils of the bush often advanced rapidly, due to the relative cheapness of the land and the shortage of labour that ensured high wages. Despite this, fewer and fewer people were attracted to the Swan River. One reason for this was the often negative presentation of the colony in the British press, which showed the colony as a sink of drunkenness and iniquity, mosquitoes, flies, heat and disease. This image dogged the Swan River from its very beginnings. A cartoon published in Britain during 1830 depicted the lot of those landed on the beaches at Fremantle awaiting scarce and expensive passage upriver to Perth. It showed a derelict shanty with a pub sign above reading, 'The Swan Tavern', poverty-stricken and drunken settler families and the hulk of an emigrant ship wrecked on the sands.[5] There are accounts of entire families camping here for months, along with their possessions, including china, cutlery and pianos. Some took one look at the barren, uninviting place and promptly sailed elsewhere.[6]

The Swan was a free settlement, but it was not an easy or comfortable place to make a new life. By the 1840s there were more people leaving than arriving. In 1845 not a single immigrant stepped ashore at Fremantle. The settlement was in a state of economic crisis that threw its future viability into grave doubt.

Swan River settlers had long debated the possibility of convicts being transported from England. To survive and to develop further, the struggling colony needed infrastructure: roads, bridges, buildings. To get these things they needed something of which they had very little: labour.[7] They petitioned the British government for the introduction of transportation to the Swan. They wanted convicts whose passage and costs were paid for by the British government and who would work hard for nothing. They did not want hardened criminals and they did not want female convicts. Their efforts were successful and, on 1 May 1849, the Swan River was classified a penal colony by the British government. The first 75 convicts, accompanied by 50 pensioner guards, their families and a number of bureaucrats under the command of a Comptroller-General of Convicts, arrived on board the *Scindian* on 1 June 1850.[8] Twenty-one years to the day after the colony had begun with such high hopes and ideals of free enterprise, it now succumbed to the provision of government-funded criminals.

Reactions to this event were mixed. While most recognised the need for something drastic to be done, many were concerned at the introduction of convicted criminals into their small community. The value or otherwise of transportation to the colony remained a contentious issue for the full 18 years of the system's operation. A satirical song of the time, sung to the tune of 'The Campbells are Coming', sums up the mixture of amusement and concern with which the first convicts were greeted:

The Convicts are coming, oho!, oho!
What a curse to the Swan! What a terrible blow!
No – devil a bit – don't fear, my old bricks,

How much we may learn, if they'll teach us their
  tricks.

The Convicts are coming, oh dear, oh dear!
Don't button your pockets – there's nothing to fear;
For surely no exile would venture to thieve,
When away from the prison, on a Ticket of Leave …

The Convicts are coming, huzza, huzza!
If you want to pick locks, they will show us the way.
Do we think to cut throats or to blow out men's
  brains,
They'll show us the mode, if we'll only take pains.

The satire ended with a swipe at Earl Grey, Secretary
of State for the Colonies:

The Convicts are coming, huzza , huzza!
Three cheers for the Convicts, and three for Earl
  Grey!
Three cheers for the Swanites and nine for each
  man,
Who devised and perfected this glorious plan.

Seventeen years later, when William Sykes and his
companions arrived aboard the second-last convict ship
ever to land in Western Australia, there was no cheering.
In fact, there was not much interest at all. By then the
convicts had become a normal and accepted aspect of
colonial life. The massive Fremantle Prison had been
built to house them, along with a number of other public
buildings, roads and public works to benefit the colony.

The transports were taken to Fremantle Prison, its great limestone walls by then already greying into the foreboding fortress it remains today. Once inside they were washed, barbered and issued with their uniforms, including the parti-coloured workgang uniforms that ensured that the convicts stood out among the colonial population whenever they were labouring outside the prison walls. Convicts' rations were basic but adequate and included bread, meat, potatoes, salt and pepper, tea, sugar, milk and rice or oatmeal on Mondays and Fridays. They were also given regular issues of soap and soda for the cleansing of their clothes and bodies.

The transformation of the free Swan River into a penal colony necessitated the building of substantial institutions of incarceration, the 'Convict Establishment', as it was officially known. Almost as soon as they arrived, the second cargo of convicts had been sent to work on the early preparations for the building in October 1850. Over the next few years, work on the prison proceeded in fits and starts as masons, carpenters and other tradesmen, whether free or bound, were often scarce. The prison's two wings and central chapel section were not completed until 1859, although one wing was occupied in 1855. This building, capable of housing a thousand inmates, was a self-contained miniature metropolis, with its own workshops, offices, stores, halls and chapel. There were 240 cells but only eight smelly toilets and legions of cockroaches. The Establishment was also equipped with the grim necessities of convict discipline, solitary confinement, a good supply of cat-o-nine-tails for flogging and, the ultimate punishment, a gallows.

The prison soon acquired a grim reputation, some of which is reflected in its folklore. Numbers six and sixteen were shunned: a 6 was said to represent the hangman's noose and 16 the noose and gallows pole. Unlucky 13 features in the 13 stone steps that lead from the gallows pit and there are 13 spaces between the beams on the roof of the gallows. The drop from the trapdoor to the floor of the gallows pit is exactly 13 feet.[9] With such macabre architectural mathematics it is not surprising that the aura of despair still clings to the prison, even since its decommissioning in 1991 and subsequent development as a heritage and dark tourism site.

As usual with public works, the budget more than doubled by the time the prison and a number of necessary subsidiary works, such as a jetty and barracks, was completed. Even so, Fremantle and its citizens did very well out of this substantial project, so much so that Fremantle developed at a more rapid rate than Perth. The seat of power in the colony languished up the river, far away from the comings and goings of commerce and crime that established Fremantle as a solid city in its own right.

Still, the wisdom of the transportation program was proven as the colony's finances gradually improved. By the mid-1860s it was possible for the Swan River to think itself a success once more. Buttressed by the reassuring mass of Fremantle Prison, the colony had become a little more relaxed about its criminal class. But not too relaxed.

When the arrangements for transportation to the Swan had been agreed between the colony and the British government it was understood by the colonists that those convicted of the more heinous crimes would not be sent to the fledgling free community. At first, this was the case. But as the years went on, the character of convicts sent declined markedly,[10] as the make-up of the weight of woe aboard the *Norwood* shows. It was not only those whose crimes were of violence and brutality who were feared, but also those who conspired against the state. Political prisoners were as great a source of concern to the colonists as were common criminals.

Even though the *Norwood* brought the next-to-last convicts – and some of those who came last on the next convict ship had a part to play in this story – discipline was rigidly maintained and zealously applied. This was notably so under the command of Governor Hampton, a man with experience of the notorious depths of the Van Diemen's Land penal system. Gangs of chained convicts were a common sight in Fremantle, Perth and outlying regions such as the developing area of Bunbury, around 100 miles south of Perth, now safely pacified of 'savages'. It was here that William Sykes and John Teale were sent in late August 1867.

Aboard the *Wild Wave* and under the command of a single warder, Sykes, Teale and 16 other convicts sailed for Bunbury and the Vasse River area. As well as the human cargo, the ship carried the usual range of supplies and foodstuffs that formed the backbone of colonial trade – sugar, tea and brandy, together with sundry other items in demand. Like Fremantle, the township of Bunbury had done well from the arrival of the convicts. It had a hiring station for renting out convict labour to the settlers who could afford it and it had a thriving mercantile export business in timbers, including jarrah and sandalwood. And it was a favourite sailortown for American whalers who frequented the settlement so often and expansively that American dollars were as welcome as local currency in the public houses and other businesses. From this outpost of administration, trade and small-scale iniquity the newly-arrived William Sykes and John Teale were sent to work with almost 100 other numbered men building the road from Perth to Albany, the major settlement in the south.

The four poachers were beginning now to be separated from each other. Henry Bone and John Bentcliffe, still lodging together, sailed north to Champion Bay. They would be set to work in the minerals industry being developed there under very primitive conditions. Both were due for their tickets of leave in only seven years. Bone seems to have remained in this part of the colony until his death at Geraldton in 1895, working on the roads and in the mines.[11] Bentcliffe received a conditional release in 1885 and worked at Champion Bay in the usual broad range of unskilled and semi-skilled jobs, including as servant, miner, shepherd and, as William Sykes would also become, a well-sinker. Bentcliffe's ultimate fate is unknown. It is possible, though perhaps unlikely, that he returned to England after the expiry of his sentence.

Far to the south William Sykes and John Teale were blistering their hands with the road-building party in the dense forests along the Blackwood River section. Even though convicts usually preferred road gangs, with their minimum of discipline, this work and the conditions under which it had to be done were not to the liking of William or his mate. After a few months they absconded to the developing settlement of Bunbury. There was nowhere else to go in the alien vastness of this place and the two were soon caught. Charged with mutinous and insubordinate conduct on 26 November, they were returned for two further months of gang labour and had their tobacco ration stopped for six months, a moderate sentence.

Similar acts often brought imprisonment on starvation rations and a flogging with the lash.

The two poachers were separated after their return from Bunbury. Teale's record indicates a number of minor and more brutal acts of violence, followed by a serious accident while a member of a survey party. The accident may have left him with a lasting disability as his subsequent record includes remissions for good behaviour and 'clemency'.[12] As did Bone and Bentcliffe, he would also end up in Geraldton, getting by as a labourer, a general servant and a shepherd.[13]

William worked satisfactorily, it seems, for the rest of that year, mainly on the Harvey Road. But he did not take the time to write to Myra, even though he was allowed to send one letter every three months. Receiving no word from William, Myra was deeply troubled, as her first letter to him in the colony shows. When Myra had sent her box of 'articals' to her husband, she had ended her accompanying letter with a plea:

Be sure to write and let me know if you have recd the box for I shall not be easy in my mind until I hear from you again ...

But she did not hear from William for a very long time. And even then it was only through his family that she had any contact with her transported husband at all.

William arrived at the Swan River in mid-July of 1867, but Myra had no word from him for a year and three months. On 20 September 1868, Myra wrote from Masborough in answer to a letter she had at last received from William dated 5 July that year. Although some parts of this letter are missing, Myra was clearly at her wits' end with worry and lack of information:

Dear Husband I was glad to heir that you were well and in good [probably 'health'; part of page torn away]

I thought that soemthing had happened to you because their was no letters for me

She is not happy that William has sent her letter care of his family, a relationship that will come under increasing strain as the years go by:

and I was much further put about when I received your letter when it was a week amongst them before I got it

Despite writing a diary of the voyage, William did not think or bother to send it back home for Myra and the children to read. Not that its brevity would have been very informative, but it would have been the thought that counted:

Dear husband when you write again send me word what sort of a pashege you had when you were going out and send word whither you got that box I sent you when you were leving this country for you never said in your letter whither you got it or not ...

Myra had been wondering and worrying about the box of 'articals' for over a year. Had the lovingly selected, expensive and carefully packed box reached him? Had he found it useful? What sort of a voyage did he have? The questions were many. And not only from her, but from the children and from their friends and acquaintances as well.

Myra goes on to give William the news from home:

*all send their kind love to you and Edward
Huttley and his wife sends their kind love also and
your daughter Ann is in place and doing well and
Alfread is working in the [indecipehrable] mill and
he gets 10 pence per day*

*Ann Thurza Alf William[s] sends their kind
love to you but William has got long white curly
hair and he was not called William for nothing for
he is a little rip right ...*

Despite her irritation with William's family, no doubt
worsened by the financial and social disparity between
her family and that of her husband's brothers and sisters,
Myra is careful to write that

*your Brothers and sisters sends their kind love to
you ...*

After the personal and family business, Myra turns to
local news. This is closely related to William's situation.
Even though some of the letter has been torn away, it is
clear that Myra is describing another affray between
poachers and keepers, not unlike that which got William
transported:

*This took place on Lord Warncliffs Eastart the
Keepper was Shot.*

This affray involved a man named Beardshaw,
presumably known to William Sykes. The consequences
of the incident included a suicide:

*Berdshaw's Father took it so much to heart that he
went and through himself on the rails and the
trains past over him and Kiled him*

Myra's brief reference to this case obscures the fact that it was an even bigger local event than the Silver Wood affair. On the night of 11 December 1867, half a year before Myra sat down to write to William, there was a 'desperate encounter' between poachers and keepers on Lord Wharnclife's estate near the village of Pilley.[14] Beardshaw was one of a group of poachers who had been surprised by Lord Wharncliff's keepers. The usual fight ensued, ending in the death by gunshot of a keeper. On the information of Beardshaw's father a man named Gregory was eventually apprehended for the murder. The elder Beardshaw was described by his wife as 'very low-spirited' and 'very uneasy about his son, who was arrested for complicity in the Pilley murder'. On the day of his death Beardshaw had wandered along the canal towpath for many hours and had then gone to the Rotherham railway line near Iron Bridge. Here, he laid his head on the rails. The train driver felt no change to the motion of the train but Beardshaw's body was found beside the track, his head between the lines.[15]

As with the proceedings against William Sykes and his companions, the trial of Gregory and the other surviving poachers elicited enormous local sympathy and unrest. According to the *Sheffield Daily Telegraph*, 'The amount of sympathy manifested for the man charged with being concerned in the murder ... is almost unprecedented in the history of crime.'[16] The article went on to say that 'Among the lower classes generally, and those of poaching proclivities in particular, it is believed the keeper provoked his own destruction.' Sympathisers met to compose and distribute through local public houses a printed appeal for funds to secure the poachers a quality defence and 'for the support of their wives and children, who are left destitute and without any aid to support them'.[17] On 10 February the *Telegraph* reported that Gregory, until then a fugitive, had surrendered to the police. He was taken from the police station accompanied by 'a great number' of friends and relations, 'between fifty and sixty persons', who shook the accused man's hand 'over and over again'. When the train arrived to take the police and their prisoner to Wakefield 'the eager crowd pressed round him, hugging, shaking hands, kissing and crying'.[18] The people of Gregory's village, Shire Green, were losing one of their own.

Gregory, and probably the other members of his gang, was well known to William Sykes and company, though perhaps not especially cordially. A notorious poacher, Gregory had given evidence against William and the others during their murder trail. He purchased the nets that the Silver Wood poachers had used from Teale the night after the affray and had been involved in the sale of Bone's dog to a man named Platts, also a witness – if an inebriated one[19] – at the Silver Wood trial.

This murky tale of poaching, murder, betrayal and suicide highlighted the local networks of the poaching fraternity and the refusal of many to condemn men such as Gregory and Sykes, despite their illegal actions. Many blamed the now almost ritualised inevitabilities of these affrays on the game laws. A correspondent to the *Sheffield and Rotherham Independent* even drew the attention of editor and readers to a long-ago poaching affray of 1819, saying, 'It bears a striking resemblance in point of time, place, and incidents, to the late poaching affray and murder of Lord Wharncliffe's keeper ... In fact it seems the same tragedy reproduced, with scarcely an alteration.'[20] He provided the paper with a report from the by-then defunct *Sheffield Iris* in which almost exactly the same events occurred close to 50 years before, in much the same location and with the same fatal consequences for a keeper.

Beardshaw and Gregory were lucky. They were eventually found guilty only of night poaching and received, respectively, sentences of 18 and 15 months hard labour. They heard this sentence with 'unmistakable signs of relief'.[21]

We cannot know with certainty what William made of this news. He probably nodded grimly to himself and put the letter carefully away in his few possessions. He was still on the road gang near Bunbury and was still suffering the loss of his tobacco issue. Even though he had only served a few years of his sentence and had been in the colony for a much shorter time, all this talk of keepers, poachers and lords' estates would already have been starting to seem distant and unreal, as would Myra and the children. Now it was William's companions of crime and their keepers who would be the reality of his life and labour.

10

Rebels and Rangers

> Western Australia is a vast and unknown country,
> almost mysterious in its solitude and unlikeness to any
> other part of the earth.
>
> John Boyle O'Reilly, *Moondyne*, 1879

Building roads to and from Bunbury, often in chains, was the best a Swan River convict could hope for. But it was not a pleasant experience. Just how unpleasant we know largely by a coincidence of history.

A few months after William Sykes and the other transports on the *Norwood* made landfall an Irish political prisoner, or Fenian, named John Boyle O'Reilly was also marched into Fremantle Prison. O'Reilly had been guilty of little active subversion, though he had plotted much. Following a brief career as a journalist, in 1863 he enlisted as a trooper in the 10th Hussars, then headquartered in Dublin. Within two years he had been recruited by the clandestine Irish Republican Brotherhood (IRB), a forerunner of the modern Irish Republican Army (IRA). Participating in the preparations for a planned uprising that never took place, O'Reilly was arrested along with most of his co-conspirators in February 1866. After a trial he was sentenced to death by firing squad but this sentence was commuted to 20 years penal servitude. With 61 other

Fenians O'Reilly was transported to Western Australia aboard the *Hougoumont* in October 1867.

Sixteen of these men, plus O'Reilly himself, had been members of the British army and were segregated from the civilian Fenians and the common convicts. When advance news of this Irish weight of woe reached the colony, segments of the Swan River community went into a panic. Just as they had in 1849, they feared that the dreaded Irish, especially those with military training, would murder them in their beds The concern was especially high in Fremantle, where the Fenians were to be held. So great was the consternation, and heightened as it was by threats from some quarters to prevent the Irish disembarking, that disciplinarian Governor Hampton had his residence moved from Perth to Fremantle in an effort to calm the more excitable colonists.

When they did arrive, on 10 January 1868, the entire complement of convicts and Fenians was disembarked at dawn and marched in chains through Fremantle to the grey prison that William Sykes and his companions had entered just a few months before. They then underwent the same initiation into servitude. Each was bathed, cropped, barbered and examined by a doctor. Their physical and personal details were recorded and they were issued with the regulation summer clothing: cap, grey jacket, vest, two cotton shirts, one flannel shirt, two handkerchiefs, two pairs of trousers, two pairs of socks and a pair of boots.

O'Reilly and his companions were now probationary convicts. If they behaved themselves for the remaining half of their sentence, they could be granted a ticket of leave, a dispensation allowing them to live and work much as any free colonist as long as they reported regularly to the magistrate. For the manslaughterer Sykes, this similitude of freedom would be a long time coming. For the political prisoner O'Reilly it would never come.

Like William Sykes and John Teale the poachers, John Boyle O'Reilly the revolutionary was, from March 1868, soon sent to work on the road making around Bunbury. Surviving records are sketchy, but it may be that he had contact with the gang that Sykes laboured with, though he was subsequently employed on other tasks elsewhere in the area. There were over 3220 and twenty convicts in the colony at this time,[1] though only a hundred or so on the road gangs in the Bunbury area.[2] Later in his life O'Reilly would publish a now-classic novel, *Moondyne*, based on his experiences in this part of Western Australia, a work he dedicated to 'the interests of humanity, to the prisoner, whoever and wherever he may be'.[3] In it, and through some of his other writing, can be discerned something of the hard life that Sykes and his companions lived.

The summer months were hot and dry; even in the fiercest part of the day, temperatures of 40° Celsius and more not uncommon. The convicts had to continue clearing the giant gums and iron-hard jarrahs, one of the colony's major exports and also in great local demand for private buildings and public works. These were then cut into smaller sections, parts of which were used to line the road, while the remainder provided useful lumber. The ground had to be levelled off or filled with rubble and the road surface pounded to something approaching evenness. Every task was carried out with hand tools of the most basic kind for nine hours every day – day in, day out.

In *Moondyne*, O'Reilly provides some evocative details of the conditions. He begins by describing the bush and the work of the free sawyers:

> *During the midday heat not a bird stirred among the mahogany and gum trees. On the flat tops of the low banksia the round heads of the white cockatoos could be seen in thousands, motionless as the trees themselves. Not a parrot had the vim to scream. The chirping insects were silent. Not a snake had courage to rustle his hard skin against the hot and dead bush-grass. The bright-eyed iguanas were in their holes. The mahogany sawyers had left their logs and were sleeping in the cool sand of their pits. Even the travelling ants had halted on their wonderful roads, and sought the shade of a bramble.*

He goes on to contrast this with the lot of William Sykes and his fellow convict toilers:

> *All free things were at rest; but the penetrating click of the axe, heard far through the bush, and now and again a harsh word of command, told that it was a land of bondmen.*
>
> *From daylight to dark, through the hot noon as steadily as in the cool evening, the convicts were at work on the roads – the weary work that has no wages, no promotion, no incitement, no variation for good or bad, except stripes for the laggard.*

Food was basic – kangaroo, cockatoo, possum and whatever else could be foraged from the ancient forests. Accommodation was usually a tent, sometimes a crude hut. Flies, mosquitoes, gnats, snakes, ants, spiders and the many other strange and frequently venomous creatures of the Western Australian bush added to the discomfort and uneasiness of men from the soft green fields and woods of England. Even poachers were not well prepared for this type of outdoor life, so the absconding of William and Teale in search of some respite was not surprising and was a common event in the road gangs.

Although the July 1868 letter William sent to Myra while he laboured in these conditions is lost, it seems from her reply that it is likely he told her none of these things. Nevertheless, when she wrote to him 16 months later on 4 November 1869, she provided a good deal of news about family and friends. But already time and separation were beginning to introduce the inevitable emotional distancing of Myra and William. The slightly stiff and formal opening of Myra's letter betrays the effects of over a year of having to get on with life in Greasbrough:

> *Dear husband I take this opertunity of writing you these few lines to let you know that me and all the Children are all well hoping that when you receve this letter you will be in good helgth as this leves us all at present …*

During this time the rancour between Myra and William's family had worsened, deepened by William again sending a letter for Myra care of one of his sisters:

> *Dear Husband it has been three weeks since I hard that their was a letter came to your Sister and I did wente to the post office to see whether it was right or not and I found out that their had been one but*

*I have never seen it yet and Ann had seen whether
hir Ant Bacer [Aunt Beccy, Rebecca] would not let
hir see the letter but She said that she would let me
nor hir see the letter . . .*

Myra is understandably upset to be told that she
cannot see a letter from William. And so are the
children. She writes that they

*has taken it greatly to heart and they are never
done speaking about it and they never give me any
pease since but I have been waiting with the
greates pacientes till they had all sen your letter
that I might know how to write to you but they
will not give it up so the children would have me
write to you without Seeing your letter . . .*

Myra continues her justified complaint, bringing the
troubled daughter Ann into the discussion:

*but Ann is the worst of them all about it and She
is bothered greatly about it every day in hir life . . .*

Nor was it just the family anxious for news of
William. Ann was working at a public house where a
number of William's old friends gathered, just as they
had when William still walked and talked among them:

*she is serving for all your old friends in
Gresbrough they are wanting to know how you
are getting on their is some of your old friends in
the house where she is every night in the week . . .*

Still angry, Myra repeats her puzzlement at the
attitude of William's family, then defiantly and not
without a note of justifiable pride:

But Dear Hysband I have worked hur [hard] for my Children and myself Since you went I have done my uttermost to bring them up as well as any other persons Children about the place and I have done so yet thank God

The children are growing up fast:

Alf is in the pit working and Ann is place[d] and Thurza and William is going to the School and by the time I get a letter from you I hope Thiza will be able to write to you

As Thirza was around 10 years old, this suggests that she had not yet had the benefit of much education.

Myra's letter concludes with some details about the illness of one of her brothers, possibly consumption – tuberculosis – a common and fatal complaint of the era, much aggravated by the dusty working conditions in the mines and factories or simply from breathing the noxious air. Another of her brothers, Ellis, has been lodging with her at Greasbrough as work in his own area of Barnsley had been 'slack', though he had since returned as employment had picked up. With this information the letter abruptly ends.

In early March 1869, John Boyle O'Reilly, the Fenian transportee, was whisked away to freedom in the United States of America by a Yankee whaler. His rescue had been carefully plotted by the free Irish community in Western Australia, in league with elements of the Catholic church, the American-Irish community and its sympathisers.[4] O'Reilly celebrated his twenty-fifth birthday in the middle of the Indian Ocean on his secret voyage back to England. From there, under the noses of those authorities who badly wanted to re-capture him, he made his way to freedom and a glittering future. In America he was influential in plans to free the Fenians remaining in Western Australia five years later.

At Easter 1874, six of O'Reilly's companions were also rescued from bondage by an American whaler, the *Catalpa*, an exploit still celebrated in the Western Australian Irish community and commemorated in a well-known ballad that makes no bones about its sympathies:

Come all you screw warders and gaolers,
Remember Perth Regatta day.
Take care of the rest of your Fenians
Or the Yankees will steal 'em away.

The verses tell the – exaggerated – story of the bold rescue of the Fenians:

All the Perth boats were racing,
Making best tack for the spot,
When that Yankee sailed into Fremantle
And took the best prize of the lot.

In fact, the *Catalpa* went nowhere near Fremantle Harbour, laying off Rockingham, far to the south. When news of the escape reached the authorities they hastily ordered the colony's only armed vessel, the *Georgette*, to undertake a pursuit of the Yankee whaler, which proved ineffectual:

The Georgette *well-armed with bold warriors*
Went out the poor Yank to arrest.
But she hoisted the star-spangled banner
Saying 'You will not board me, I guess'.

This satirical ballad concludes with the verse:

Now they're landed safe in America
And there will be able to stay.
They'll hoist up the green flag and the shamrock
'Hurrah for old Ireland', they'll say.

The politics surrounding the fate of O'Reilly and his rebellious companions were a *cause célebrè* of the time, resonating with the more romanticised aspects of the Irish struggle against English oppression. The correspondence files of the Colonial Office during this period are full of letters from respectable members of the British middle classes urging the release or pardoning of the Fenians. Particularly, there was a considerable amount of correspondence relating to O'Reilly's case.[5]

But while Irish political prisoners had contacts, networks, affiliations and access to funds, Yorkshire poachers had no such advantages. William Sykes, John Teale and the thousands like them had few representations made on their behalf to the powers of authority at the Colonial Office. They remained behind to hew the wood and till the soil of the Swan River, serving out their time and dreaming of flight.

Escape is a constant obsession of those constrained in prison camps. A penal colony, even one as relatively subdued as the Swan River, is little different. There are continual mutterings, plots and rumours of plots. Escape attempts were a continuing feature of prison life throughout the Fremantle Prison's grim history.[6] Occasionally, as O'Reilly and the other Fenians proved, someone succeeds, inspiring legend and emulation. While such successes are few and far between, and the failures many, there was, during William Sykes's life as a convict, another colourful Swan River colonist who personified the dream of escape.

Joseph Bolitho Johns was a 22-year-old Welsh transport when he arrived in 1854. Earning a conditional pardon in 1855 he took up the business of catching stray horses, returning them to their owners for the rewards offered on such valuable assets. Operating in the Toodyay area Johns was arrested on suspicion of causing the horses to leave their rightful owners and 'catching' them in his horse traps at a place called Moondyne Springs. He was arrested and imprisoned, but while awaiting trial he escaped. Recaptured, the horse-stealing charges were dropped but he received three years imprisonment for gaol breaking. Released in 1864 he was returned to gaol inside a year, this time with a 10-year sentence. The charge was killing an ox with intent to steal the carcass. But the working party he was sent to labour in could not hold him long and Johns, now developing something of a legend among the convicts and settlers, reflected in the nickname 'Moondyne Joe', escaped again.

When they caught him this time, the bushranger was given a further year in chains. Bound fast in irons within a cell, Joe, still in irons, almost escaped again and was placed in another, supposedly escape-proof cell in the prison refectory. It was only another 10 days before he disappeared from here and enjoyed several months of freedom in his old stamping ground around Moondyne

Springs. In September 1866 he was captured again and placed in a specially constructed escape-proof cell in Fremantle Prison.

Here, in solitary confinement, on a bread and water diet and in an enclosed space with little light or air, he became so ill that the medical authorities said he would die. So Joe was taken out of his cell every day and left in the corner of the prison yard by himself, watched closely by a guard and kept isolated from all contact. When he recovered, he was put to work breaking stones. Eventually, he smashed a large pile of rubble behind which it was difficult for the guard to see what was going on. On 8 March 1867, all was as usual: the guard watched Joe's pick rising and falling behind the pile of rubble, occasionally checking verbally that Joe was still there. He was. What the lazy guard could not see was that Joe's pick was not attacking rocks but a loose stone in the prison wall. As the heat of the day faded the guard could see Joe's cap over the rubble but could not get an answer from his call – 'Are you there, Joe?' Seeing the cap, the guard assumed Joe was having a break and neglected to walk over to check until knock-off time at 5 o'clock.

Of course, when the guard went to get Joe he found the cap, a broad-arrow patterned jacket propped up on a couple of picks and a large hole in the prison wall. Joe had breached the stone barrier, left his prison clothes behind and wriggled into the garden of the prison superintendent's house. Then, he simply strolled through the superintendent's front gate which, fortunately for the convict, happened to be open.

Pandemonium erupted as prison authorities and the police scrambled to catch the great escaper once again.

Governor Hampton, who had called Joe an 'immense scoundrel' and publicly boasted of the escape-proof cell, was especially displeased, a fact that only increased the pleasure of the broad community of settlers and convicts, for whom Joe had now added another triumphant chapter to his legend. In the streets they sang, to the tune of 'Pop Goes the Weasel':

The Governor's son has got the pip,
The Governor's got the measles.
Moondyne Joe has give 'em the slip
Pop, goes the weasel.

Moondyne Joe had become a colonial Robin Hood.[7] His song and story were still much in the air by the time William Sykes arrived at the Swan River. He would have heard various, increasingly embellished, versions of the story, many of which are still told today.

After absconding from his 'escape-proof cell', Joe remained at large for another two years; he was eventually recaptured at a local vineyard on 25 February 1869, drunk according to some accounts. He served another lengthy sentence – without escaping – and, in time, followed William Sykes down to the Vasse River region on a ticket of leave. But by then William had long departed.

As far as anyone knows, William Sykes, John Boyle O'Reilly and Moondyne Joe never met. But the facts and folklore of the bushranger and the Fenians were living legends. They seemed to leave open a small chink in the prison walls that held at least a promise of something that just might be, one day. But not now. For the moment William Sykes the poacher and convicted manslaughterer must serve out his time and wonder, as did his fellow transport John Boyle O'Reilly, if this was the end of his life.

While the ill-educated William was not skilled in the written word, the literary O'Reilly cried out his own fears and those of all transported convicts in verse written at this time:

Have I no future left me?
Is there no struggling ray
From the sun of my life outshining
Down on my darksome way?

Will there no gleam of sunshine
Cast o'er my path its light?
Will there no star of hope rise
Out of this gloom of night?... [8]

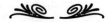

There is a record of one other letter written by William during this year, 1868. Where or to whom he sent it is unknown. Perhaps it was another message to one or more members of his own family – Elizabeth, her husband Charles or perhaps to his successful and prosperous older brother, John. But it was not to Myra. Nor had she written to him. Far away in Masborough, Myra had problems of her own.

11 *The Long Years*

it harte breaks me to write like this
if the prodigal son cud come Buck to his home wons
more
tahre woold be a rejoicing ...

Myra Sykes to William Sykes, March 1872

While William was being broken into a life of penal servitude in the Western Australian bush, back home in England Myra was struggling to make ends meet and bring up the children. Without a husband to work, and to supplement their basic diet with an occasional rabbit, Myra had a difficult task ahead of her. She could certainly not expect any money to be coming from William. So she needed employment to put food on the table and clothe the children. She had to see to the children's other physical needs, too: their clothes, their health and also to such education as was available. Fortunately, the older children, Ann and Alfred, were of working age and Myra no doubt depended heavily upon them, though, as her letters reveal, neither was totally reliable as a source of income.

William probably wrote to Myra again late in 1871, possibly even as early as 1870. Myra's reply is dated 9 March, presumably in 1874.[1] She had been working hard and long as a laundress and her letter is weary and care-worn. By now the ties of affection and loyalty are being strained by time, distance and the demands of getting on with life. She has not much word from William:

dear Husband I been long In writing to you I hope you will forgive I receved you letter and was plesed with it I think you mite send me more word wot your doing ...

Despite the next sentences, in which she says that all at home are well, she later tells him that she is not well herself and that some of the children have also been ill. She asks William to exercise some fatherly guidance to young Alfred, who is rapidly growing up, obviously a little too quickly for Myra to handle. She is especially concerned about his liking for public houses, especially at the relatively tender age of 13 or 14 years:

I want you to send a line to Alfred he is geting up likes to go to the public But is not a Bad lad to me ...

There are also more additions to the family:

I expect you will be a grandfather of to Wenn this Letter arrive at you ...

which seems to be a reference to Ann's twins, after the birth of which she returned to work, though, according to the census for that year, she was still living at home, had lost her place as a housemaid and was unmarried:

Ann on Again she not very good Luck lost a dule of time from binn poly ...

Young William, now five, had also been poorly, but was looking better, Myra said. Then she asked if William ever writes to his brother, Joshua. It seems that Joshua has raised the possibility of some political intervention in

William Sykes's case should Mr Anthony Mundella be elected for Sheffield. He is elected, but we hear no more of politics until the very end of William's story.

Now Myra seems to loose control of her emotions:

it harte breaks me to write like this if the prodigal son cud come Buck to his home wons more tahre woold be a rejoicing …

A few lines further on Myra recalls her last sight of William at the Leeds assizes:

and you mencend about Lucking young I thort you did when I saw you at leeds my hart broke neley wenn I felt your hand bing so soft ..

There is a line about the fine-looking girl that the 11 or 12-year-old Thirza, also still at home, has grown into, followed by a wistful recollection of Myra's own birthday, 17 March:

as for my self I not lucking very well at present

This is followed by some news of relations, including work in the Wombwell main coalmine at Barnsley, where around 1200 workers were employed above and below ground:

Alfred is in the Woinbel main pit and Ann Husband and my Brother Ellis Alfred full week 19 6 pence he minden ganger …

It seems from this that those back home were in work and managing as well as could be expected. The wayward Alfred was apparently working as a ganger, or foreman, in the pits, according to the census in the capacity of a horse driver. Employment in and around the pits was important in the continuing family connections between Myra and William's children, Ann's 'husband' and Myra's family. Another relation was 18-year-old Frank Sykes, a miner. He was lodging with the family in April 1871, as was another young miner, 23-year-old William Waterham, apparently Ann's 'husband'. It was this barely glimpsed network of relations, friends and work associations that helped sustain Myra through the long years of desolation.

Myra concludes this letter by raising a hope that would sustain her and the children – and perhaps William – for many years, the possibility of him one day returning to England. This hope would eventually become one of the many ironies of William and Myra's story. For now, though, such a hope was, as Myra said herself, only a wish:

Ann Husband says He Wood Work hard for you to come hom if it cud be Done and my and my [sic] Dear Husban I sends my nearest and Dearest Love to you and all the children with A 1000 Loves and kiss wish we may meet again ho that we cold in this World

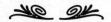

It was now seven years or more since Myra and William had last seen each other. Back home, tales of the events in Silver Wood and their aftermath were being handed on to a growing generation and becoming legend. But William Sykes was no hero. He was not the stuff that heroes are made of, but nor was he considered a villain by those who loved him or by those who belonged to the same social class. To these people his fate was more like that of the martyr. In their eyes, William and his poaching companions had done no wrong. To the contrary, poaching was a widely admired pastime, economic supplement and submerged social protest in this part of the world. Nor did many think of William as a murderer. In the moral order of this time and place those who defended the rights and resources usurped by the rich and powerful were fair game themselves. The death of a keeper was regrettable, but the stupid bugger should not have been doing the job in the first place. These, at least, were the lines along which would run the popular wisdom muttered in forges, pits and pubs by men who, despite their lowly station, were well aware of the vested interests and power politics of industrial England. The suggestion of political intervention in William's case, raised hopefully in Myra's letter as having been mooted by Ann's husband, strongly echoes the family's concern for the possibility of repatriation, bolstered by the continuing unhappiness within the community about the severity of the sentence.

These political resonances had no relevance to William Sykes, Swan River convict. He continued labouring with the Bunbury road gangs at different locations throughout the district. He cut drains in the swampy ground around Harvey and worked on the Capel Bridge at Bunbury. On 18 March 1873 he was charged with drunkenness, an old habit perhaps, that would also plague him in later years. Other than this, no more is heard of him until his road gang is transferred back to Fremantle in September 1874.

The next year, 1875, was a busy one. On 12 January 1875 William wrote to Myra. Although this letter is lost, the gist of it is clear from Myra's reply of 11 April. She begins in her usual, slightly formal manner:

> *Dear Husband I writ these few lines to you hoping to find you well as it leaves us at present*

Then, as she often did, Myra returns to the theme of the letters from William that she never received. Whether he ever wrote them, Myra believed he did, a suspicion aroused by the fact that William had addressed his letter to a Kit Royal:

> *I dont douted but you have rote a many letters that I never heard tell of I wonce was th[r]ee years and had not had a leter ...*

Then Myra tells of the terrible news she had received:

> *your relations said that you was Dead I went to Rotherham townshall and asked if they knew wheather you was dead or not one of the police sade he heard you was dead ...*

Poor Myra was now convinced that her dear husband was dead, the family news casually confirmed by the authority figure of the policeman:

> *I put the chealdren and my self in black for you my little Tirza went to the first place in deap black ...*

Having dressed herself and the children in mourning clothes, Myra was at once devastated and relieved to discover, through William's favoured sister, that she had been misinformed. Not only had this letter been directed to William's sister Elizabeth, but to add insult to injury, Elizabeth had also refused Ann leave to see the letter:

> *then I heard that your sister Elizabeth had got a*
> *letter from you my daughter Ann went to see if*
> *they had told her that you was all rite and (and)*
> *they told her that ther leter had gone to Sheffild*
> *she could not see it ...*

Myra mentions that the Bible and copy of *Robinson Crusoe* that Elizabeth had purchased for William during the trial are now in the possession of William's brother, John. He is living at Barrow-in-Furness, she told William, though she was clearly not in contact with him as she does not know his address or, in the speech of the time, 'the directions'. William obviously was not concerned with either book in his new colonial life. And, if he had read it, the castaway theme of *Robinson Crusoe* may have been rather too close to his own predicament for comfort.

Myra then moves on to complain of William's other sister, Rebecca, whom she lent the considerable sum of five shillings:

> *I lent Rebacca five shiling to go to Leeds with and*
> *never gave that back ...*

From this point the letter starts to ramble, reflecting Myra's state of mind:

> *I had to do the best way I coud for my cheldren*
> *and my self ...*

Then she returns to her thoughts of William, who she again refers to as a prodigal son as well as a castaway husband:

> *Dear Husband cant express myself to you but I*
> *hoap to see you wonse more seeted in corner I will*
> *the beest for you if it coms to pass...*

Myra may by now be suffering from the effects of what is now identified as depression:

Some days I feel pretty chee[r]ful and others very sad But I think it is owing my age …

Then, of course, news of the children. Ann is pregnant once more, though there are problems here as well:

I must tell you tha Ann geting Again for A nother and am sory to tel you that he is not one of the best of husban

Later in this disconnected letter, Myra goes on to say of Ann's partner:

I don't think he is veary fond of work he is a unculted man

This turn of events must have been an especially sore disappointment to Myra who, in an earlier letter, had been glad to tell William of Ann's 'husband's' statement that he would do all he could towards having William repatriated.

But there are bright spots. Myra then proudly tells of the other children. Alfred is taller than his father's 5 feet 6½ inches. Thirza is very solid, an attribute that in those times and circumstances was considered a healthy sign, and William, Myra's favourite, is also growing tall:

my Alfred I beleve is toler than you pepel is seprsed with him Thirza I belive she not far off 11 stone william nist [nice?] boy he does not luse a inch of is ight

This letter ends with some news of and best wishes from old friends, especially the constant Edward, or

Ned, Uttley and also mentions a relation of one of the convicted poachers, Luke Booth, still living locally. Although they did not expect to see William Sykes ever again, the local people kept him in their living memory.

Six months or so later, William received a surprise in the form of a letter from his son, the younger William Sykes. Dated 20 October 1875, it begins with bad news:

> *Dear father I write these few lines hopeing to find you better than it leaves us at present my mother as been very ill and me my self and I am a bit better ...*

Soon, the letter becomes a young man's cry of pain for the father he barely knew:

> *Dear father we think you have quite forgot us all my sister Ann takes it hard at you not writing oftener ...*

And later:

> *Dear father you never name me in you letters but I can sit down and write a letter to you now ...*

Young William ends:

> *we all send kindest and dearest love to you and God bless you and 1,000 kisses for our Dear father from your Dear son William*

Such a letter and the sentiments it contained must have torn at William Sykes's heartstrings, no matter how hardened and despairing he had become.

Elsewhere in his son's letter, the elder Sykes heard news of his two grandchildren:

sister Ann as to nice boys the oldest is a fine little fellow

and of his other children:

well I mys tell you what a stout young man my brother Alfred as got and Thirza is a stout young womman poor Ann is very thin ...

William junior goes on to tell how he often plays with his Aunt Rebecca's boy and how she often says that the younger William resembles his father.

Whether William senior was aware of William junior's next piece of news is unknown. He tells his father that Rebecca's oldest boy, also named William, has been dead for 15 months.[2] The transported felon also learns that Greasbrough has undergone quite a few changes in the eight years since he left, including the erection of a new Congregational church where young William goes to school, no doubt to the satisfaction of his Uncle Charles and his Uncle John who is still resident at Barrow-in-Furness where he continues to do very well for himself.

In one section of this letter, the younger William conveys a recurring question from Myra as to whether the authorities would permit him to have a picture, presumably a drawing, of his family

Dear father Mother would like to no if they would alow you our likeness

though there is no evidence of any likeness ever having been produced.

In the same envelope as young William's letter came a hasty note from Myra. The near-indecipherable handwriting indicates that she was not well in body or in mind and very worried about Ann's domestic problems. It seems that Ann was pregnant for the third time and Myra was not looking forward to having to look after her during the pregnancy:

Dear husban I am grvd to my hart A bout my Ann I have had her Both times of her confindments and Ly shee gating on gain

Then Myra scribbles what were possibly the last words to pass between herself and William Sykes:

We hall send our nearst and dearst Love to you with A 1000 kiss Dear Husband you must excuse writing

William may have received a letter from Myra the following year, but if so, it has not survived. What these few lines do tell us is that Greasbrough and the surrounding districts were expanding rapidly along with the general expansion of Rotherham and Sheffield. Life was hard, but it seems that there was work for those willing and able to take it. While Myra was by no means well off, between her efforts and those of the older children and, assisted perhaps by her own family (though probably not by William's) – and possibly another[3] – she was able to get by.

Her illness would have undermined the fragile balance of working life and family life. There were no social security benefits or sick leave in those days so she would have been thrown back onto the generosity – or otherwise – of friends and relations. As her letter makes clear, though, all was not well with Ann and her marital arrangements. The combination of her unnamed illness and Ann's troubles no doubt brought about her distressed emotional state during these difficult years.

They were difficult years for William, too, as we know from the rediscovery of letters he sent to his family in 1876. He had now been separated from home and loved ones for a decade. On 10 March that year, William wrote to one of his sisters, probably Elizabeth, and his brothers, John and Joshua. The letters were written on two sheets of notepaper and sent together in the same envelope, now missing. These are the first, and only, words we hear directly from William in Australia, and they are mostly unhappy. They tell us that he was a troubled man.

In his letter to Elizabeth he at first talks of being in good health:

> *thanks be to God for it and not the dicetfullness of men on Earth*

the latter a reference, no doubt, to the circumstances of his trial and imprisonment. He then begins to apologise for the trouble he has brought upon the family but seems unconvinced by his own sentiments:

> *I do not think that I have given you as mutch trouble as you have caused me*

In an ironic twist, given Myra's complaints about his failings as a correspondent, William is upset that his apparently numerous and sometimes lengthy letters to his family have received no response.

> *I have tryed hard to hould a corespndence with you all and I have heard of you receiving my letters but no anseers and it is that what Greaves me to my Hart*

William then goes on to address Joshua:

My Dear Brother your mother I do believe whas
my mother and shee was a good mother and a
Father likewise to me God rest her soul

After this acknowledgement of his mother's goodness, William suggests that she may be working on his behalf in the afterlife and seems to suggest that some 'vilen', perhaps Woodhouse or one of the other false friends, may be coming in for some retribution. He says that, despite his problems,

I never enjoyed better health myself with all the
vileny

The letter continues, asking Joshua to contact him and send his address:

dear brother I want you to rite to me will you and
send me your directions

William then regrets that the police had not allowed him to see Joshua at Rotherham before he was tried, apparently believing that this would somehow have allowed him to escape his punishment:

if I had a seen you before I got tryed I should not
have had any Sentence at all and thay new that
too: and my sisters nows what they said to them
at Wakefield

Something similar was intimated to William's sisters at Wakefield Prison, presumably while they were visiting him there before his removal to Portsmouth. He then gives Joshua a titbit of information relating to a highway robbery and murder of which he has knowledge, in the hope that Joshua might somehow benefit from the reward

I wrote one letter with twelve pages in it let me know if any of you got it will you it contained a little information about a Hiway robery and murder and I do not want no police nor detective to get ould it as ther was a reward out at the time

Added between these lines is the name of the alleged offender and the assurance that

I have nothing to do with it only I was tould all about it by one of the party the saem night it happend and I always kept it a seacret

William then says that he is

the villind no more

and implies that this is his main motivation for passing on this valuable piece of criminal information.

Moving on from this odd communication to his apparently upstanding and hard-working brother, William Sykes turns to his older brother, John. William seems to have had no word from or of John until William the younger had mentioned John's visit in his letter of the previous year. The letter to John begins on a seemingly positive note, with William repeating what he had read in his son's letter about John's visit to Greasbrough and that he was pleased to hear that John was in good health. The news, he writes

gave me grate plesure to hear it as I have often wondered if you wher living or dead

But this turned out to be a lead-in to what is at first a sarcastic, then pathetic, cry from the heart:

I could not think if you whear alive that you whould not rite to me

From here the letter speedily moves to bitter recriminations of what William considers to be John's refusal to communicate with him:

I allways thought I had a brother in you but no

He recalls the night that John had visited him at Rotherham, probably after the first trial, and what had passed between them:

I culd call to mind that night when you came to se me at Rotherham and wat you said and then never come to se me no more

William cannot understand John's actions and is in great emotional pain, repeating his tortured words:

I should not have done so to you no i should have come to se you John I should have come to se you John I should never have done as you have

William concludes with the standard correspondent's farewell, now given additional weight and poignancy by what he has just written:

no more at preasent from your afectonate Brother W.S. still untill death part us John I remain so

Not once does William mention Myra.

A Conditional Freedom

I can but ask that I may, like others, have a trial on my ticket of leave and I feel assured you will have no future cause to regret the leniency.
I am Sir
Yours respectfully.

William Sykes requesting a ticket of leave, 1876

Apart from the pains of separation, William's situation eventually improved a little. Around October 1875, he was sent to Newcastle (now Toodyay) Hospital. Newcastle was the successor settlement to the earlier Duigie, said to mean place of water in the local indigenous dialect and pronounced 'too-jee' (as it still is by some locals, though the usual pronunciation is 'too-jay'). Toodyay was established in 1837 when the colonial government built facilities there. Between 1860 and 1861 flooding of the Avon River led to the abandonment of the official site; another town was created a few miles upstream. This new settlement was named Newcastle Town at first, then quickly became known just as Newcastle.

In this small but bustling centre of policing, land administration and farming, William Sykes worked as a servant to Dr Mayhew. The medical man had arrived in 1867 aboard the migrant ship *Palestine*, together with his wife, a teacher with rather a difficult personality by all accounts. Mayhew was eventually appointed district medical officer, a position he was to hold for many years, earning the affectionate local name 'the Old Doctor'.[1] William must have proved a satisfactory worker because on 26 January the following year, 1876, Mayhew wrote on behalf of William to request he be granted a ticket of leave.

After they had served some of their sentence in a reasonably obedient way, convicts were able to apply for this document. It conferred a form of parole that allowed the holder a limited but desirable degree of freedom from the eye of the authorities. In William's case, as a lifer, he would need to have served at least six years and nine months as a 'Very Good' prisoner (the second-highest category after 'Exemplary'). As Mayhew's letter shows, William would have been something of a disappointment to his moralising brother-in-law, Charles Hargreaves. He had not managed to progress from probation to ticket of leave in the minimum time. But by now, with his overseer's help, he was able to present a reasonably good case.

William's request was, presumably, dictated to Dr Mayhew by William himself. If so, Mayhew gave it a polish, a firm, educated pen-stroke and ensured that it was in the kind of grovelling prose the Prison Department favoured for communications from convicts asking for favours:

> Sir
>
> *I have the honour to forward my name to your notice for favourable consideration having now completed 10 years 1 week & 13 days probation out of 12 years 6 months &15 days – I have been*

a contractor about 2 years and during the whole
term of my probation have had but 2 reports for
breach of rules.

I have been under Dr Mayhew now for several
months and I hope [to?] say that I have given him
every satisfaction.

I can but ask that I may, like others, have a
trial on my ticket of leave and I feel assured you
will have no future cause to regret the leniency.

I am Sir
Yours respectfully[2]

The combination of William's comparatively good record and Mayhew's advocacy paid off. On 14 September 1877, a ticket of leave was granted to William Sykes, upon which he was discharged.

William had managed to put by a respectable sum of money earned from his gratuity. He had £10 in the savings bank at Newcastle. In July the following year he withdrew the lot, plus interest.[3] It seems that he needed the money to establish himself in the well-sinking business, a hard but profitable trade in a thirsty colony.

Sinking wells was a necessity, even in close proximity to natural water sources. The original surveys of land for the colony around Perth and Fremantle had taken this into account by laying out long, narrow blocks with access to the essential waters of the Swan and Canning Rivers. But when settlement spread north, south and inland, this neatly-regulated system generally gave way to a more *ad hoc* occupation of smaller or larger areas of land. Often the only sources of water were underground springs or flows that could only be reached by sinking artesian bores. These had to be dug through the sand

and rock, frequently to very great depths. Like the road gangs, this was hot, hard and very unpleasant work, but we know that William undertook this labour, in partnership with one or more other men, for quite a few years after his ticket of leave was granted.

One of the letters in the kangaroo-skin pouch concerned William's business dealings.[4] Dated 14 May 1879, it was from a James Ward, a pioneer sheep farmer at Goomalling, about 30 miles from Newcastle.[5] Ward had employed William and one of his partners to dig a well for him. Apparently, there was a dispute about the agreed rate. The letter writer admits that he was wrong and that the rate William and his mate had quoted – 5 shillings a foot for every 5 feet dug – was correct. Presumably, this gave William some satisfaction, as well as some more money.

Unfortunately, the combination of money and relative freedom on his ticket of leave does not seem to have been good for William. Probably believing that all contact with his family, his children and with Myra was now severed, he gradually lapsed into a deepening trough of despair and what would today be called binge drinking.

In November 1879, William received a caution from the police for being drunk. It was more than 18 months before his name appeared again in the official records but that probably only means he was not caught again until 1 June 1881, when the next entry occurred. That day he was found drunk and absent from his lodgings and fined 10 shillings. On 28 October, he was also drunk and absent from lodgings, a misdemeanour for which he was punished three more times the following year – in February, March and May. On 6 October he was caught 'out after hours'.

These events were almost certainly only those occasions on which William was apprehended. The alcohol problem – or 'the grog', as the convicts would have said – probably put him into Newcastle hospital for a month in 1883. When released he was in a poor state of health. After this, perhaps as a result of illness, he seems to have sobered up. He received his conditional release in 1885, which meant that William was now able to go anywhere within the colony, except the northern gold regions, but could not leave Western Australia until his full sentence had expired. For William Sykes, that meant never.

In the year William received his conditional pardon, payable gold had been discovered far to the north in the Kimberley region of north-western Australia. There had been finds and rushes before, resulting in the whole colony living in a perpetual state of expectation that a major strike would be made at any time. There were even rumours of rich reefs in the Toodyay area. Whether William had ambitions to strike it rich or not, he missed his opportunity because soon after receiving his conditional release, he went to work on the railway.

Construction on the rail link between Perth and its agricultural hinterland had begun in 1881; by 1885 the line had reached the town of York. In 1886, in response to persistent representations by the people and businesses in and around Toodyay or, as many still called it, Newcastle, a spur line was built through the junction of Clackline. It is possible that William may have worked on this construction, which generated a large demand for labour. He was then employed mainly as a maintenance man, or ganger, in and around Clackline Junction.[6] He was certainly performing these duties in 1887, a role that probably suited his preference for a low profile very well. When Alexandra Hasluck asked old timers around Toodyay if anyone could recall anything of William Sykes, no one could place him. He was not a man to make himself noticed, a useful skill for a poacher, and for a convict on conditional release.

By contrast to William's arrival almost a quarter of a century before, the Swan River Colony was now booming. When transportation was introduced the hope had been that the cheap convict labour would establish a firm economic base. This hope proved to be an illusion and transportation ceased in 1868. Those old lags, such as William, still had to serve out their time, of course, and they did it through the sluggish years of the 1870s and 1880s. But from the mid-1880s the discovery of gold in a number of places in the colony, especially in the Murchison, Yilgarn and at Kalgoorlie, Boulder and Coolgardie, provided the economic and population boost that the colony needed and the basis of its resource-dependent present. The population of Perth was just over 6000 in 1884. By 1891 it had reached almost 10 000 and by 1901 was almost 44 000.[7]

Now, living quietly in his small wooden railway hut at isolated Clackline, William may have read and re-read the little stock of Myra's and young William's letters. Or perhaps he never looked at them again. But he did feel the need to preserve them and at some time, perhaps during the year at Clackline, he made or procured the kangaroo-skin pouch in which the documents were later found. Apart from these few grubby slips of scrawled paper, the only other comforts he had were a dog and a rifle, the traditional accompaniments of the poacher.

But he was no longer the English poacher. His time in the Swan River Colony had made him one of a class that characterised colonial Australia and that has remained as a mainstay of the great Australian legend. William Sykes, coal miner, foundry worker, poacher and transported felon had become a bushman. The short stories and poetry of 'Banjo' Paterson, Henry Lawson, 'Dryblower' Murphy and a hundred like them are peopled with rugged, independent males living alone in a bush hut with only a dog, a rifle and a few regrets to keep them company. Comforts were few and consisted mainly of the grog and bad food. Not surprisingly, many of these men lost their reason and became 'hatters', a type that features in many a bush yarn and that was canonised in Lawson's story, 'The Bush Undertaker'. Lawson, who spent some time in Western Australia on two occasions – in 1890 and 1896[8] – wrote of a crazed old bushman recovering the mummified body of an old mate. He takes one too many pulls on the brandy bottle and is chased by a flock of black goannas that may or may not be an hallucination.

The characteristic bushman was a tough, lean, taciturn individual who depended on himself for as many of his few needs as possible. He was used to getting by on not very much and making do with very little – somewhere to roll a swag, some tucker, a dog and a good knife were nearly all that was necessary to sustain a harsh life in the unwelcoming bush of Australia. Personal possessions and the emotional life of the inner man were given scant regard. This pared-down existence and stoic outlook suited the self-contained soul of William Sykes.

After 23 years of exile in a harsh and distant land, William had little to look forward to for Christmas 1890. As far as we know he had neither been writing nor receiving letters to or from the faraway place that was still, however faintly, home. He had been unwell for weeks now and the advancing heat at this time of the year was only making him feel worse. A few days after Christmas, on 29 December, the Newcastle police learnt that William was lying ill in his hut at Clackline Junction, unable to help himself. They sent somebody out to bring him into the hospital. He was diagnosed with a hepatic ulcer and chronic hepatitis of around two months' duration, probably the legacy of his hard drinking. Four days into the New Year of 1891, William died.[9]

Convict 9589 no longer had any need of numbers, nor of the £1/14/10 found in his pockets, nor of his gun, his dog or the kangaroo-skin pouch that enfolded a bundle of old letters. The Inspector of Prisons and the Superintendent of Poor Relief were informed; they duly filled in the appropriate paperwork and organised a coffin and burial at government expense, though not much of it, just £2/15/-. The dog was sold and the proceeds, plus the £1/14/10 were remitted to the authorities towards the cost of burial. At the end of her *Unwilling Emigrants* Alexandra Hasluck described the convict's last resting place:

> *William Sykes has no monument. He was buried in a nameless grave in the cemetery at Toodyay [Newcastle], at the back of the Anglican section, outside the consecrated ground, in a part reserved for convicts, paupers and suicides, on the slope of a hill covered in summer with dry yellow grass.*[10]

Nine months after he was laid anonymously away the police also sold William's gun, the £1 it fetched going to the Inspector of Prisons. In the end, the death of William Sykes had cost the good citizens of the Swan River Colony precious little.

In one of her earliest letters to William, before he had been transported across the seas aboard the *Norwood*, Myra had written:

> *If you have the chance to earn Any money in Australia you must save it all up and I will do the same, that if there is a chance of our rejoining you we may be able to do so.*

Myra never lost hold of the hope that she and William could some day be reunited. She clung to it throughout the decades of silence and worry, and she passed it on to her children as well. To one of the boys, at least. Even though it is not clear which of Myra and William's sons initiated the action, it was almost certainly William's namesake, the 'little rip' and writer of the anguished letter to his unknown father in 1875 who visited the Reverend Beard at Greasbrough Vicarage one autumn day in November 1890. Young William Sykes asked the clergyman to use whatever influence his position held to approach the government for the return of his father to England. The family hoped that William would at least be allowed to die in the land of his birth and among those who loved him.

In a clear hand, the obliging vicar wrote to The Right Honourable G Mathews Esquire, local member of parliament:

A parishioner of mine has been to see me relative to his father William Sykes who, at the Christmas Assizes at Leeds in 1865 was sentenced to transportation (I believe) for life ...

He repeated the case made to him by the representative of the Sykes family:

He has 2 sons and 2 daughters and they would gladly pay his fare home if the Government would permit him to have his liberty.

Beard went on to state the mitigating factor in William's case, as put to him by the family:

I believe that his sentence was owing to his complicity in a poaching affray which resulted in the murder of a keeper.

The vicar was no doubt following the wishes of the family in underlining the word 'complicity' in his petition. Together with their peers in the local working-class community, they held to the belief that William had only played a part in the death of Lilley. Woodhouse's treachery, as far as they were concerned at least, was a sure sign that he had struck the fatal blow and had perjured himself in return for freedom and the pieces of silver represented by the £350 reward. While these burning beliefs did not appear in the official correspondence from Reverend Beard they were certainly the emotional fuel that powered the family's resolve.

Mathews duly set the wheels in motion. On 5 February 1891 a Whitehall bureaucrat wrote to the governor of Western Australia, informing him of the petition for Sykes's release and asking for details of his record during the last quarter century or so of his obscure life.[11] The writer (his signature is indecipherable) stated that the original trial depositions could not be found and provided details of the case from newspaper accounts and 'other documents in the Home Office'. These were rather less favourably couched than those of the family and the vicar or even the more carefully phrased request of the local member:

> *Sykes was one of a gang of poachers, and he and another man took the most active part in an affray in which a game-keeper was beaten to death with sticks; Mr Justice Shee, who presided at the trial, remarking in passing sentence, that few persons would have disagreed with a verdict of 'murder'.*

In fact, quite a few people had disagreed with that verdict, including, most importantly, the jury, which had refused to convict Sykes of murder. However, the Whitehall bureaucrat allowed a glimmer of hope in the following paragraph:

> *Sykes is now 61 to 63 years of age, and it is perhaps unlikely that if allowed to return to this country he would relapse into crime ...*

Whether the faint optimism of the Whitehall bureaucrat would have been justified, no one would ever know. Even as the letter writer carried out his official duties, William Sykes had already been dead and buried a month. The bare facts were laid out in the officialese of the colonial secretary's Office Minute Paper No 551/91 of 5 February 1891. From the Home Office on the Subject of the Release of Wm. Sykes to return to England, the minute contained a note from the superintendent of prisons to the governor, together with a copy of William's 'prison reports'. The note quoted another minute from the resident magistrate at Newcastle (Toodyay):

the Superintendent of Poor Relief conveys the information that Sykes died in the hospital at Newcastle on or about the 4th, or 5th, January last and that his effects are but of trifling value.

The note was dated 14 March 1891. Documenting his extinction, these minutes flying high above the now uncaring station of William Sykes were also the last official recognition of his existence.

By now, news of William's death would have reached Myra, the children and William's family. They might have prayed that it was another false alarm, but this time it was officially confirmed. The family's grief and mourning would have been no less bitter for the separation of time and distance. But at least that was an end to all the long years of suffering, the waiting and the worrying, the long and ever-longer gaps between William's letters and the sheer need to just carry on, to get by.

It seems that neither the Western Australian nor the British government made any attempt to return to Myra those 'trifling' effects of William's that had not been sold. Perhaps the family tried to find out about them, perhaps not. In any case, there is no evidence. So it came about that Myra's letters, William's diary of the *Norwood* and a few other items in the kangaroo-skin pouch of an old lag came to be lost behind the shelves of the Newcastle Police office until that day in 1931 when they were found once more.

Unlike the convict Magwitch of Dickens's *Great Expectations*, William Sykes never returned to England. But, as we now know, while William's story came to an end in the heat of the Western Australian summer, Myra's continued in a northern industrial town on the other side of the world.

13

The Sting in the Tale

Dear father you would hardly know
Greasbrough now if you seed it …

William Sykes the younger to his father, 20 October 1875

During all the years William Sykes had been cast away in the struggling Swan River Colony, Sheffield and the surrounding area expanded massively. The population of the region trebled in the last decades of the century, buoyed by a seemingly insatiable world demand for steel products. The number of souls said to be living in Sheffield in 1831, a year before Myra was born, was just under 92 000. When William died in 1891 there were almost 410 000 and the villages and fringe suburbs and villages of his earlier days were enveloped by the growth of Sheffield and Rotherham. Factories, forges, railways, roads and seemingly endless rows of cramped houses had multiplied across the fields and streams, obliterating almost all traces of the woods and wildlife the poacher and his mates had once known. In 1895 much of what remained of Silver Wood was chopped down,[1] leaving a sparse remnant, itself increasingly pressured by roads, farming and residential development

But the costs of this development were higher than the rewards. Industrial blight, ferocious smog and widespread water pollution accompanied some of the deepest poverty and squalor the Industrial Revolution had spawned. A description of Greasbrough at this time is provided in J. S. Fletcher's *A Picturesque History of York*:

at Greasborough ... the full tide of industrial life surges upward again. This place was famous for its coal-pits 100 years ago, and is still distinguished by its sombre aspect and smoke-laden skies ... [2]

Fletcher also provides a description of nearby Masborough, where the happier part of Myra and William's marriage had been spent so many years before:

But as the traveller reaches Masborough ... he passes within the absolute boundary of the industrial bee-hive, and may regard himself a stranger to everything but smoke and flame, the clank of steam hammers, and the clang of machinery, until he leaves the southern edge of Sheffield behind him. [3]

Health, sanitation, nutrition and education were all poor as well. The privately supplied water of the area was an ongoing problem until, in 1888, local government finally succeeded in taking it over.[4] People managed as best they could, depending on a combination of their own exertions, friends, family and whatever help institutions were able to provide. From her first surviving letters it is clear that Myra has a host of burdens to bear other than the transportation of her dear husband. In March 1867 her mother was very ill. Myra has been invited to the home of William's brother, Joshua, but has not been able to find the time to go. A few years later one of her brothers, Alfred, suffered from the same unnamed disorder as that of another of her brothers, the now-deceased Manuel.

Money is a perennial worry. Myra is unable to journey from Sheffield to Portsmouth for one last sight of William because she does not have the money – she has had to pay the rent. Myra says that she is willing to spend that amount of money as long as she can be sure of seeing him. If not, 'it will be a serious loss to me situated as I am'. She promises to come if he has not sailed before the next 'reconing'. But she will have to come alone as

none of them say anuthing about coming them-selves, or assisting me to do so either so far

another of the numerous references to the strained relations between her and William's family.

In April 1867, Myra walks to Sheffield 'in the hope of getting a good shut knife for you' but, oddly in a city famous for its cutlery, is unsuccessful. Later in her letter she hints that her failure to obtain the knife had more to do with money than availability:

If Saturday had been pay day I might perhaps have been able to get a trifle more for you.

As well as raising the children, Myra was a working woman and she needed every penny she could get. Without the income from Ann and Alfred's jobs – he was getting 10 pence a day, a good wage, it seems – life would have been even more difficult for Myra and her large family.

Life was a continual struggle for most working people, especially for a woman raising four children by herself. Myra's letters tell a fragmentary but intelligible tale of her success in raising the children without their father. Alfred and Ann, the older children, are in work in 1869, by which time the family has moved to Greasborough. Alfred is now in the mines and Ann continues in domestic service, possibly in a lodging house. The younger children, Thirza and William, are attending school and Myra has had her brother Ellis and his son lodging with her while they search for work, 10 miles away from their home town of Barnsley.

At this time there is also a faint and brief glint of hope for William's case. In a number of her letters Myra mentions the hopes of some of William's friends and family to find a way of having his situation reviewed by the authorities. The election of 1868 throws up a candidate named Anthony John Mundella, resident in Nottingham and keen to represent the trade unions, Reform League, teetotallers and some dissenting religions. An important plank in Mundella's platform is his opposition to the game laws.[5] There was little rioting at election time that year, though the elections of 1865 and that of 1880 led to a reading of the Riot Act and the summoning of the army. There is optimism that if he gets in, 'Mondeller', as Myra spells his name, may do something for William, a suggestion that local feelings about the case was still strong. It is also hinted that William's successful brother, Joshua, has access to Mundella, or at least the political machinery that put him into Parliament as the member for Sheffield. But no more is heard of this.

In that year, there is a piece of news that Myra may have written to William. It is news that explains many things, including William's denial of his marriage upon arrival at Fremantle and the worsening relationship between Myra and William's family.

On 16 July 1868, one-and-a-half years after her last known contact with William, Myra gave birth. The baby was named Frederick.

How Myra's transported husband learnt about this, we do not know. A disbelieving and despairing William may have read of the birth in the letter he received from Myra written in September 1868. After a moment or two of incomprehension, perhaps he ripped the frail page to shreds, casting it angrily away; a sheet of paper is missing from that letter. Perhaps Myra did not tell William at all, hoping that somehow the news would not travel to the other end of the earth. Perhaps he had word from his own people. The only certainty is that in William's surviving correspondence to his family there is no mention of Myra, or of their children, or of hers.

The record is silent and continued to be silent about Frederick Sykes. Myra's later letters are full of news about the doings of Ann, Thirza, Alfred and William, but in these letters Frederick does not exist. Yet this last child grew up in Myra's household alongside the children of William Sykes. He was certainly there in 1871 when the census records his presence at 'The Village', Greasbrough, as the three-year-old son of the head of the household, Mirah[6] Sykes. He was still living there 10 years later, now said to be aged 12 and already earning a much-needed crust for the family as a labourer. By 1891 23-year-old Frederick had joined his brothers and many of his other collier kin in the hot black pits.

It is not hard to imagine what Myra's in-laws made of these events. The respectable and pious Unitarian Charles Hargreaves, no doubt backed up by Elizabeth, would have delivered numerous homilies. John, the rapidly progressing elder brother, may have shaken his head ruefully and counted his blessings that he and his family had not come to such a pass. Joshua's reactions were probably similar, though perhaps not so severe. Myra's family may well have accepted such realities with the equanimity of those who expect little from life and are not surprised when they receive less. It was Myra's mother, who was living in the family home at that time, who informed the registrar of Frederick's birth.[7]

Myra's emotions must have been bitter-sweet. Fiercely loyal to her convicted husband she had nevertheless been unfaithful to him as he rotted in the mosquito-infested forests of Western Australia's south-west region. The joy of a baby boy was mixed with the disapproval, perhaps even the disgust, of William's family, and the no-doubt busily wagging tongues of friends and neighbours.

Not once does any suggestion of these emotions appear in Myra's letters. Among the local and family news, the insistent requests for more correspondence from William, the loving good wishes of herself and the children – in Myra's mind now including Frederick – there is never a mention of these things. Myra presented to William and to the world, a person of stoic, even steely, determination, dedicated to doing the best she could for her children and herself in circumstances of the most distressing and difficult kind.

Who was Frederick's father?

The birth certificate contains the details of Myra, her address at the time – 39 Midland Road, Kimberworth – the address of her mother and the sex of the child. But the section headed 'Name of Father' remains poignantly blank.

Was Frederick the product of a liaison springing out of Myra's loneliness? Was he the result of a brief, misjudged moment? Did Myra come to some harm without the protection of a resident husband? Was Frederick the child of the man for whom she kept house and who was to become her second husband, Charles Mitchell?

Like many of the other mysteries raised in this story, there is no solution, only a few fragments of fading notepaper that offer more questions than answers.[8]

In her next, only partly dated letter to Toodyay, Myra gives William the news that he is about to be a grandfather again. Ann is pregnant, although she has been unwell. Another of her many brothers, Herbert, has a drinking problem and she herself is 'not lucking very well at present'. Myra and William's eldest son, Alfred, also has a drinking problem and Myra asks William to write to him about it. Alfred is earning good money in the pits, along with Myra's brother Ellis and Ann's 'husband'. At least, that is how Myra described William Waterham, the 23-year-old 'Lodger' who was present in the house on 2 April 1871. Myra was living at 'The Village' in Greasbrough by this time, together with all five children, William Wareham and another lodger, Frank Sykes, an 18-year-old coal miner, possibly the son of William Sykes's older brother, Joshua. Myra had work as a laundress, though Ann was a 'Housemaid out of place'. The 13-year-old Alfred drove horses at the same colliery where William Wareham worked, alongside Myra's brother, Ellis.

A few years later, in her letter of April 1875, Myra tells William of the devastating experience of believing him dead and of dressing her 'little Turza' in 'deap black', only to then discover, gratefully, that he was not dead. Myra blames this on William's family and his habit of writing to them rather than to her. She is also bitter about lending William's sister Rebecca five shillings for travel to Leeds and not to have it repaid: 'I had to do the best way I could for my cheldren and my self.' Myra says that she is emotionally up and down, probably correctly ascribing this to her age, now 43. She also tells William that Ann is pregnant yet again and that her husband is 'a unculted man' who seems to be shy of work.

In October that year, Myra is too ill to write to William. Young William takes up the pen to tell him that Alfred and Thurza are both stout, while 'poor Ann is very thin'. He is proud to tell his father that he attends the Congregational church school in Greasbrough, which has developed so fast that William would 'hardly know Greasbrough now if you seed it'. He wonders why his father never writes to him. In an undated letter, probably of 1876, Myra writes briefly that she is 'grvd [sic] to my hart A bout my Ann'. Ann is pregnant again and, as on the previous two occasions, much of the burden of care will fall on Myra.

There are no more letters from Myra after this. The long years of hardship and loneliness had left their mark upon her life. But she had succeeded. Without the male breadwinner she managed to bring up the children, clothe them, feed them and get them an education. At what cost to her emotional well-being can only be imagined. During most of the correspondence between herself and William, Myra had usually reported that she and the children were in work, though we know from the census record and Myra's letters that such employment was uncertain. This, together with some support from William's and – perhaps, though she rarely mentions them – her own people, would have supported the transport's family.

By 1881 Ann and Thirza had left home, though the boys were still with Myra. They were now living at 3 Scrooby Street, still in Greasbrough, and had the 50-year-old John Evans, an unmarried labourer from Elsecar, Yorkshire, as their lodger. Myra, now 49, had no work but, it seems that between the lodger and the wages of the boys, she was getting by.

By the time of the 1891 census Myra, even though she could not know it, had her revenge on William's forsaking of her when he had refused to acknowledge a wife on arrival at Fremantle. In the column provided for recording marital status, Myra indicated that she was of no status, not even a widow. She was now living at Church Street in the home of the widower Charles Mitchell, officially as his 'Housekeeper'. At the time of that census she and Charles were living in the house with William Sykes junior, the American-born Elizabeth and their three-months-old child, another grandson for William Sykes, though it was too late for him to know that.

William's family went on with their lives. So did Myra's. She was a strong, resourceful woman and one who managed to mostly preserve her emotional balance in circumstances that would have defeated many – and did. When William died in 1891, Ann was 37, Alfred was 34, Thirza 32 and young William, 'the right little rip' who resembled his father most of all, was 26 years old.

Myra was 59. She had spent almost a quarter of a century and more than half her adult life trying to maintain a relationship with a husband amputated from family, home and country for a stupidly savage act. She had not only held a family together for that very long time, but she had also seen them all through whatever education was available to them and the only kinds of employment to which people of their period, place and circumstance could reasonably aspire. She had done so without benefit of a welfare state, with relatively little help from William's family and only a little more from her own. Myra had done everything that could reasonably be expected of anyone in her unenviable position, and more. With William's death there was no longer any need for her to pen those difficult letters beginning 'Dear husband', or to feel guilty when she did not, or perhaps could not.

Now Myra had a chance for a brief moment of happiness. On 19 November 1892, she married Charles Mitchell at St Mary's in Greasbrough. Mitchell was a local man who had described himself as 'living on his own means' at the 1891 census. The marriage records show that he had been a miner. Myra was listed as a widow.

Although we cannot know if Myra's last few years of life were happy, it would be good to think they were. Hopefully, they were lived in a cheerful house with a loving husband, surrounded by her children and grandchildren as well as the new generation of her maternal family, the Wilcocks,[9] the idyllic happy family of Victorian England. After half a century of hard work, worry and pain, if anyone deserved two contented years, Myra did. It was not much of a return, but it was better than nothing.

Though, if Myra's second marriage was a happy one, it was of short duration. Mitchell died the following year, leaving Myra alone once more. The remaining two years of Myra's life are without surviving documentation. We next hear of her through the church that had played such a central role in her life. For a fee of tenpence h'penny Myra Mitchell was buried at St Mary's in Greasbrough on 20 December 1894, three days after she died of bronchitis and cardiac syncope. She was 62 years old.[10] Her perfunctory death notice appeared in the *Rotherham & Masbro' Advertiser* two days later. No mention was made of William Sykes.

Myra and William's children lived on. Perhaps Ann's domestic and marital difficulties faded away and she enjoyed a happy and long life, loved and supported by her numerous children. We do not know if this was the case, but thanks to the research of Dennis Taylor we know at least that little Thirza did marry. Her husband was a Joseph Outram, with whom she had four children. They named one of the girls Myra. A family photograph reveals Thirza as a woman of about average height and not particularly stout. She is seated beside Joseph, a man worn to hollowness by a lifetime of hard work. Her face is pale, her hair dark, parted in the middle and drawn tightly back. It is an open face, though Thirza's eyes look as though they hold secrets. She wears the standard dark dress of Victorian family photographs: raised to the collar with a white ruff, pinned at the throat with a brooch. Her hands cradle, or perhaps contain, a belligerent boy of about five or six years old, with his hand on the family dog, a villainous-looking mongrel, probably spoiled with affection by a young and growing family. Joseph died in 1908, but Thirza lived on to a ripe old age, through the First World War and a good way through the Second, dying in her early eighties in 1942.

For the male heirs of William Sykes, young William and Alfred, the last decade of the nineteenth century and the first decade of the twentieth may have been times of change and betterment. Given the average life expectancies of the time it is unlikely that any of them lived to witness the carnage of the Great War, though Myra's fifth child may have seen that insanity, perhaps even been part of it. We do not know.

Although lost in time, there are continuing echoes of William and Myra's lives in Australia, England and New Zealand. In Rotherham the events of so many years past are still the subject of local interest. The Rotherham Library has published a booklet on the trial of the poachers for the murder of Lilley. A play based on the story has been written. Thirza's great-grandson, Dennis Taylor, has researched the family history and local records and written a novel based on the life of William Sykes.[11]

William, Myra and their families also live on in local history, in genealogical research and even in the modern-day tourism industry. Alexandra and Paul Hasluck's determination to save the Toodyay Letters and the stories they held has been richly rewarded by posterity.

From New Zealand, Thirza's descendants Clive and Jean Outram, have travelled to Western Australia to visit the presumed site of William's grave. They also attended an unusual observance inside Fremantle Prison. At a ceremony of honour on Foundation Day, 5 June 2000, the Fremantle Prison Guardians presented Clive, William's great-grandson, with a certificate in the name of William Sykes, convict 9589. A certificate was also presented, *in absentia*, to Mrs Ida Taylor, the great-granddaughter of William and Myra. The ceremony of honour is an often emotional event recognising the convict heritage of the recipients. It has been held annually since 1992, the 2000 event marking the one hundred and fiftieth anniversary of the arrival of the first convicts.[12]

It is, perhaps, the final irony of this story. William Sykes, convicted of manslaughter and transported to the colonies for life in the 1860s is an honoured convict ancestor in 2000. Who knows what William would have made of this event, enacted in the confines of the newly-sanitised Fremantle Prison, though otherwise little different from when he entered it in 1867. What would Myra have thought about this feting of the dear husband she had defended in court and laboriously written to through all the years of transportation, drudgery and despair?

The question of Myra's honouring also begs an answer. Is not her constancy and – notwithstanding the arrival of young Frederick – her loyalty worthy of recognition and reward? Does not her struggle to bring up five children without a father in the crucible of industrialism deserve at least a little of history's condescension? William Sykes may have been convicted of the crime, transported and served his time. But Myra and her children served that sentence too, like the family of every prisoner ever bound inside a gaol.

Lost Graves

Time and change have obliterated almost all traces of Myra and William. Without Myra's letters, William's brief shipboard journal and a handful of official documents, their story would have been lost to history. The humble but substantial two-up, two-down where they lived perhaps the happiest year of their lives together in Midland Road, Masborough, is long gone. The land on which it stood is now public open space where the neighbourhood children play. There is still a works operating on the site of what had been Masborough Ironworks, William's place of employment just across the road from the house.

St Mary's church in Greasbrough, the pivot of so much of Myra and William's lives and hopes, remains. It is still a place of worship for those Anglicans living in this suburb of Rotherham. But the cemetery where Myra was laid to rest has disappeared, demolished very many years ago, along with the remains of any headstones. Today it is a rather desolate-looking square of grass, relieved only by a few trees.

But beneath those trees Myra sleeps. A survey of the monumental inscriptions carried out when the old churchyard was converted to a garden of remembrance in the mid-1960s provides only one faint clue to her last lodging. Headstone number 139 marked a double grave. The carving was so weathered when the recorders got to it that they could not read the first initials or any other details. Only the initial letter of the surnames was visible – two 'm's. Perhaps Myra and Charles Mitchell lie here together, finally at rest.

If so, they are not alone. Headstone number 186 marked another double grave. It contains the bodies of the pious Unitarian Charles Hargreaves and his wife Elizabeth. He died in January 1885 aged 64. Elizabeth followed him two years later, only 61 years old. Next to them was headstone number 187, which commemorated the small remains of young William, son of Samuel and 'hant Becca France'.

A mile or two away from St Mary's, across the valley floored with railways and metalworks, is what remains of Silver Wood. The site of Myra and William's parting is a sparse, much depleted woodland. Here, the local people walk their dogs and, perhaps, stop for a pint at the sports club built in the field close by where it all happened, the club's concrete carpark hard up against the edge of Silver Wood.

At the other end of this story, at what is still the far rim of the world, there remains nothing to see and little more to tell. William's last resting place in Toodyay cemetery is still a mystery. Alexandra Hasluck was told by the Toodyay gravedigger, Ted Chapman, that there were three rows of graves in unhallowed ground beyond the official burial sites. But according to later research William Sykes was buried in the Anglican section of the cemetery. As there are no longer any relevant records extant, this cannot be confirmed. And there is also a local tradition that the grave was moved at some time.

Toodyay itself is a pleasant bush town, centre of a thriving rural hinterland and busy tourism industry. Its colonial buildings – settlers' cottages, Connor's Mill, St Stephen's Anglican church, the Uniting church and the old library are interspersed with the outposts of colonial officialdom most familiar to William Sykes. The police stables, the gaol and the courthouse are still there, attracting tourists to their restored facades and hollow interiors. The hospital where William worked and from which Dr Mayhew wrote on his behalf for a ticket of leave is gone, along with the old police buildings where the letters were first lost and then accidentally preserved for so many years. The town is full of plaques and markers informing the curious passer-by of the historical significance of this place and that. But there is no mention of William Sykes.

Through the trivial accidents of history excavated in these pages, the few fragile words of Myra and William Sykes, their children and relatives survive. Today Myra and William's letters, along with that of young William, are kept safely in the Battye Library, available to anyone who completes the appropriate forms to see, to touch and to read. The paper is sere and pauper-small in dimensions, the handwriting mostly cramped and laboured; the letters are faded, torn and smudged. Through these pathetic pieces of paper and through almost a century and a half, the loyalty of Myra to her dear husband shines on. The letters also tell of the enduring affection of William's estranged children, especially his namesake. A few thousand scribbled words of two obscure ghosts separated for almost half their lifetimes and by half a world, testify to the human spirit and, most of all, to the power of love.

The Toodyay Letters and Related Documents

All the known letters of the Sykes family, together with other relevant documents mentioned in the book are reproduced here. Spelling, punctuation and, as far as possible, the layout of the documents have been preserved. Neither Myra nor her husband was adept with pen and ink and it was a considerable effort for them to put words to paper. William had been educated at Sunday school and at a day school, a reasonable level of education for the time and place, but his later life and occupations did not provide many opportunities to practise whatever writing skills he may have learnt. Myra probably had even less formal education and it was clearly a great trial for her to write even a brief letter. Nevertheless, she persevered and when her own hand was not up to the task she had others take down her words, mainly young William, whose schooling was markedly better than that of his parents.

15 March 1867
Dear husband i rite these
few lines to you hopeing
to find you better than it
leaves us at present i have
been very uneasy sinse you did
not rite my children cried
When we got no leter. Mrs Bone
has got two leters sinse I got
one will you please to rite to
me and send me wird how
you are getting on i have bilt
myself up thinking i shall get

to you some time or another
My mother sends her best love
to you she has been very ill
but she is better at present
we all send hour kind love
to you we all regret very much
for you i hope their will be a
lighting for you yet Woodhouse
has been for giving hiself up
severl times when he has been
in drink i hope he will your
John and Emma send their
love to you we have wished scores

of time you was comeing in to the
house we should syuse you to deth
for we could like to see that
Jhon ward lives next door to

us he sends his respects to you
his wife his pius womman
she talks about you very
often Joshua Sykes has sent
word for me to go to their
house but i have not had
time to go you must not delay
riteing if you can it will ease
my mind if you can

if it ever lays in your power
to send for us when you get
abroad i would freely sell
all up to come to you if i
possibly could for health

Dear farther do pleas
to writ to is i Sends one 100
kiss for you thirza Sykes
a kiss will xxxxx
Ann Sykes sends Dear xxxxx
father i send you a 100 kiss for you
Alfredd sens kiss kinds
Love to you Masbro
Midland Road 33

Masbro' 19 March 1867
My dear Husband –
I have this afternoon received
your letter and i am glad
to hear from you – I heard yesterday
that there was a letter from
you at Park-gate and wrote off
immediately to the Governor of
the Portsmouth prison asking
him to kindly send me word
if he could what was the
latest day I could see you, as
I do not see how I could pos
sibly undertake the journey
this week, being without mo
ney, If I had received your
letter on Saturday, it was
the reconing and I would have
done my best to contrive it –
But if you do not leave before
the next reconing I will come if
I came alone for none of them
say anuthing about coming them-
selves, or assisting me to do so either
so far. I feel it as much as you do
to be very hard for you to be
where you are and Woodhouse
at liberty, but rest assured
whether I git to see you or not I
hope that when you arrive at
your journeys end you will not
forget us, for we are always

thinking about you. I hope the
governor will either send me a
reply or allow you to do so, for I
will leave no means untried to
get to see you if there is time
but if I was at the expense only
to be too late when I got there
it will be a serious loss to me
situated as I am. I feel greatly
hurt that you should send your
letters to you Brothers & Sisters
before me – for although we are
separated there is no one I value
and regard equal to you – and
I should like you to still have
the same feeling towards me,

and if there is ever a chance
of our being permitted to join
you again even though it be
in a far off land, both the
children and myself will most
gladly do so – Mr Bone has
written to his wife to get the
childrens likenesses taken for him
to take away with him I should
like you to have ours if you
are allowed the same privilige
Will you let me know? I cannot
give you up. I live in the hope of
our being together again somewhere
before we end our days – My best
love to you, the children also send

their love to you, and love and
remembrance from all friends
your affectionate wife – Myra Sykes

JOY AND HAPPYNESS OF THAT BRIGHT WORLD ABOVE

This is intended for William Sykes number 283
Portsmouth Prison

Sir
Governor of this prison Sir it is not my wish or will to
go against the rules or Regulations of this Prison and I
hope and trust through your instrumentality that
William Sykes Convict number 283 will receive this
into his hands and i hope it will not miss his heart and
i wish to inform him that his wife and children
Brothers and Sisters are all well at present for ought i
know we send our dearst and kindest respects to you
hopeing it will find you in good health, William my
advice to you is that you obey all that are in authority
over you and Let your conduct be good and try to gain
that which you have lost i mean your character let me
beg of you to pray to our heavenly father and his son
Jesus Christ to give you a clean heart and right sprit
within and then all your troubles and anxieties of this
world will be small when compared with the
Joy and happyness of that bright world above William
I hope you are aware that our Blessed Lord has
caused all holy scriptures to be written for our
learning and God Grant that we may hear and
read them and not to read them only but to do what

*they teach us and then when the swelling of Jordan
overtakes us may we be ready to meet our saviour and
him be ready to convey us through the valley of the
shadow of death to our heavenly father arms there
everlasting to dwell with him dear brother i ask you to
seek for Christian salvation which means deliverance
from something that is feared or suffered and it is
therefore a term of very general application, but in
reference to our spiritual condition it means deliverance
from those evils with which we are afflicted in
consequence of our departure from God it implies
deliverance from ignorance from ignorance of God, the
first and the last the greatest and the wisest, the holiest
and the best of beings, the maker of all things, the centre
of all perfection, the fountain of all happiness, ignorant
of God we cannot give him acceptable worship we
cannot rightly obey his will we cannot hold
communion with him here we cannot be prepared for
the enjoyment of his presence hereafter But from this
ignorance we are rescued by the salvation of the
Gospel, which reveals God to us which makes us
acquainted with his nature, his attributes his character,
his government and which especially unfolds to us that
scheme of mercy in which he has most clearly
manifested his glory it is good that a man should both
hope and quietly wate for the salvation of the Lord.
William a few more words when they was leading Jesus
to the cross and there followed a great company of
people which also bewailed and lamented him but Jesus
turning unto them said Daughters of Jerusalem weep
not for me but weep for yourselves*

*Well William in conclusion i will say a little about
the contents of your letter. i believe you said your
children was the strings of your heart i believe you
went on to say that wentworth was your place of birth
and i say let Christ be your salvation
William your brother John sends his best hopeing the
advice Given will have a good effect your sister
Rebecca sends her love to you and trusts she will see
you again before death do you part and your sister
Elizabeth sends her kindest love to you wish you to
behave yourself under your present situation and as for
me C Charles Hargreaves my desire is to point you to
the Lamb of God that takes away the sins of the world
and trust in Christ as your Physician for it is through
Him that we live and move and have our being Dear
William your brother John would give your little boy a
good school education but your Dear Wife cannot find
time to send him to school i conclude with the blesssing
of God almighty the father the son and the holy Ghost
may remain with you both now and forever amen i
trust the governor of this prison is a kindhearted Man
Charles Hargreaves Park Gate near Rotherham
Yorkshire.*

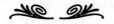

Masbro' April 8th 1867
My dear Husband –
I have this day sent off a
box for you which I hope you
will receive safely – I have
sent you all that I possibly
could and am only sorry
that it is not in my power
to send you more – as soon
as I received your letter I took
it to Elizabeth – She has
sent you two of the smallest
spice loaves and gave me 1s
towards the expenses – Then I
went to Rebecca and she
could not do anything towards

it. Emma has sent the other
spice loaf and mince pie – &
Elizabeth the testament and
tract, and John the other two
books, and the remainder I
I have sent myself – I hope
you will write back the very
first opportunity to let me
know if you have received
it. I have paid 4/6 carriage
to Bristol they will send us
word what it costs from there
to the ship and John will
pay that, I should like you
to write as often as ever you

can, and when you write next
send word whether a few post
age stamps will be of any
use to you – I walked to Shef
field yesterday morning in the
hope of getting a good shut
knife for you, but could
not meet with any of them
Sailor Bill is very well but
I did not see him, and Chas
Salt has gone into the North
and Edw. Uttley sends his best
respects to you. If Saturday
had been pay day I might
perhaps have been able to get
a trifle more for you I called
at John Cliffs they send their

love to you & Mrs [?] sent an ounce
of Tobacco – We also send our best
love to you and the children all
wish they were going in the
same ship with their Father. I
have enclosed you a list of the
articles in the box and Father [?]
encloses a packet of needles
with his respects – If you have
the chance to earn any money in
Australia you must save it all up
and I will do the same, that
if there is a chance of our rejoin
ing you we may be able to do so.

*Be sure to write and let me know if
you have recd the box for I shall not
be easy in my mind until I hear from
you again – Remaining with best
love and wishes for your welfare.
Your affectionate wife – Myra Sykes.*

MYRA'S LIST OF ARTICLES

*flanel Shirt 1
Belts 2
flanel compforter
1 anchifes pocket
2 caps
2 purs
1 comb
2 Cotton shirts and Looking glass 1
4 needles and thread
6 anks*

OLD FAVOURITE TOBACCO POUCH

Three Spice loaves – 2 lbs Cheese
One Pork pie – one mince pie
2lbs sugar – 2 tea 2 do.
Packet of Spice – quire of paper
4 books – ½ doz pipes
Bottle of Tobacco – parcel of Tobacco
Old favourite Tobacco pouch
Thread needles Buttons &c
Three bottles of ink & pens
2 Fig cakes – Apples oranges and lemons
Bottle of pickels 1¼ lbs Bacon
Alfred sends his little pocket knife

STRONG SEA ROWLING

On Board the 2d of April
Sailed from Portland the 18
head wind ruff night
the Sattedy night before
Easter and Easter Settedy
night Caut a Shark on the
21st of May a Death the same
day a funeral the 22nd
A ship came up and took
Letters the 23 a good Breas of
wind 24 A Birth on the 26th
Crossed the line the same day 26
which was Sunday
the outlandic Ocan the tropic

the medary Island the cannary
Island the peak of tinereff
along the coast of affreca
and other peak mountains
8 days brees. Steady wind 2 June
good wind 3 making preparation

for ruff wether 4 oppisit Eugener
Brassil out of the tropic 6 fair
wind not much of it
7 niggers Friday night
8 strong wind boult in the flihg
jib broke out 9 – 10 good sailing
11 Strong not in faver 14 fare wind
squaly albertrosses ollegok cape pigen
and other Birds 19 wind in faver
but very could dail and rain
very strong sea rowling dreams
very ruff night 20 dull with strong
swell on 21 Birth died 22 wet
miseruble day with fair wind
23 fare wind going well but squalls
24 and 25 changuble 26 ackedent
with the Boiler and too men
scolded July 1 sailing very fast
with squall until the 9 and
then calm and dull

Masbrough 20 September 1868
Dear Husband I take this oportune-
ty of writing you these few lines
to you to let you know that
I receved your letter dated the
July the fifth 1868 Deir
Husband I was glad to heir
that you were well and in good

[page torn]

whither I had got one from you
or not and that put me about for
I thought that something had
happened to you because their
was no letters for me and I was
much further put about when I
receved your letter when it was a
week amongst them before I got it
Dear husband when you write again
send me word what sort of a pashege
you had when you were going out
and send word whither you got that
box that I sent you when you
were leving this country for you
never said in your letter whither you
got it or not I am very sorry to be

[lost page]

Old house still and they all

send their kind love to you and
Edward Huttley and his wife

sends their kind love also and your
daughter Ann is in place and doing
well Alfread is working in the
– al mill and he gets 10 pence per day

Ann Thurza Alf William sends their
kind love to you but William has
got long white curly hair and he

was not called William for nothing
for he is a little right rip right and your
Brothers and sisters sends their kind
love to you and their was another

[torn page]

This took place on Lord
Warncliffs Eastart the Keepper
was Shot.

Berdshaws Father
took it so much to heart that he went
and through himself on the rails
and the trains past over him and
Killed him

Dear Husband
when you write again Derect
your letter to Mrs Sykes No 39
Midland Road Masbrough

Greasbrough 4 Nov 1869
Dear Husband I take this
opertunety of writing you
these few lines to let you
know that me and all the
Children are all well hoping
that when you receve this
letter you will be in good
helgth as this leves us all at present
thank God for his kindness to
us all Dear husband it has
been three weeks since I hard
that their was a letter came to
your Sister and I did went to
the post office to see whether it
was right or not and I found out
thatv their had been one but I
have never seen it yet and Ann
had seen whether hir Ant bacer
would not let hir see the letter but

She said that she would not
let me nor hir see the letter so
the children has taken it greatly
to heart and they are never done
speaking about it and they never
gave me any pease since but I
have been waiting with the greates
of pacientes till they ahd all
seen your letter that I might
know how to write to you but
they will not give it up

so the children would have
Me write to you without
Seeing your letter but Ann
is the worst of them all about
it and She is bothered greatly
About it every day in hir life
about it wheir she is serving
for all your old friends in
Gresbrough they are wanting to

know how you are getting
on their is some of your old
friends in the house where she
is every night in the week that
is in Harriss But Dear Husband
I cannot tell what they have
all got against me for I have
never yet bothered them for
nothing since you left us all
Bt Dear Husband I have work
ed hur for my Children and
myself Since you went
I have done my uttermost
to bring them up as well sa
any other persons Children
about the place and I have
done so yet thank God

We are living in Gresbrough
and Alf is in the pit working
and Ann is place and Thurza
and William is going to the
School and by the time I
get a letter from you I hope

Thiza will be able to write
to you Dear Husband my
brother Alfred is always bad
the same as my Brother manuel
was before he died and he
sends his kind love to you and
all our familey does the same
Ho and I had my Brother
Ellis and his son Lodging with
me for some time but they
went back to Bannesley
the work was slack there but
it is much better now

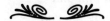

MY HART BROKE NELEY

9 March
Dear Husban I been long
In writing to you I hope you will
forgive I receved you letter
and was plesed with it I think
you mite send me more word
wot your doing I hope this will
find you in good health as
it leves us at present I want you
to send a line to Alfred
he is getting up likes to go
to the public But is not a
Bad lad to me and I expect
you will be a grandfather of to
Wenn this Letter arrive at you

Ann on Again she not very
good Luck lost a dule of time
from binn poly but he
Lucking well my littel Bill as
as been very poly he is
Better and Looks well

I want to now if you Write
to your brother Jos i have seen
ons I think cince you
went away I hearit say that
if Mr Mondeller git in the
elections for Sheffield that
he wood be abel to have some
convesation with him and
try to do something for you
it harte Bricks me to write
like this if the prodigal son
cud come Buck to his home
wons more thar woold be
a rejoicing I must tel you
that my Brother Herbit as
got very bad Brunt I
expecte as been getting Drunk
linge on the flor I have not
been to see him I must tell
you that Mr Mondeller got
in for Sheffield and I hope he
will do you good

and you mencend about
Lucking yong I thort you
did when I saw you at Leeds
my hart Broke neley wenn I

felt your hand bing so soft.
Dear Husban you wood be seprice
to see wot a grit fine lucking
girl Tirza is it will be my
Birth day on Tuensday 17 of March
as for my self I not lucking
very well at present
Brother and sister sends there
best love to you John tell
friends often ask if i ever
hear of John thay not yet
Alfred is in the Woinbel main
pit and Ann Husban and my
Brother Ellis Alfred full
week 19 6 pence he minden
genger

Ann Husban says He
Wood Work Hard for you
to come hom if it cud
be Done and my
and my Dear Husban
I sends my nearest
and Dearest Love to you
and all the children
with A 1000 Loves and
kiss wish We may meet
again ho that We
cold in this World

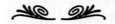

11 April 1875
Dear Husband I writ
these few lines to you
hoping to find you well
as it leaves us at present
we receved your letter dated
12th of January and was
glad to received it and we
recived your letters you directed
to kit royal I dont douted but
you have rote a many letters
that I never heard tell of I
wonce was thee years and
had not had a letter ... your
relations said that you was
Dead I went to Rotherham
townshall and asked if they
knew wheather you was dead
or not one of the police sade
he heard you was desd

I put the chealdren
and myself in black
for you my little Tirza went to
the first place in deap black
then I heard that your sister
Elizabeth had got a letter
from you my daughter Ann
went to see if they had told her
that you was all rite and
and they told her that ther
letter had gone to Sheffild

she could not see it that wan
the time you wass directed them
to your sister Dear Husband
Elizabeth fected the Bible
and Robinson crewsaw
while I was at the Leeds asices
I bleve John has them
John is living at the
barrow in farnsess in North

I donth now drections
I lent Rebacca five shilings
to go to Leeds with and never
gave that back I had to do
the best way I could for my
cheldren and my self
Dear Husband cant express
myself to you but I hoap to see
you wonse more seeted in
corner I will the beest for
you if it coms to pass
Some days I feel pretty
cheeful and others very sad
sad But I think it is
owing my age well I
must tell you that Ann geting
Again for A nother and
am sorry to tel you that
he is not one of the best
of Husban

Dear Husban I must tell
my Alfred I beleve is
toler than you pepel is

seprsed with him
Thirza I belive she not
far off 11 stone william
nist boy he does not luse
a inch of is ight but Ann she
would be cross with me if
new I sent you wird
I dont think he is veary
fond of work he is a unculted
man peter Looffield
very best respect to you he doing
well he Loves that house that Tamer
selars Ned Utley sends Love to you
My brothers and Sister best Love –
xxxxx xxxxx Luke Booth send is
respects he live at the wite
house ould Mr Crssland

[page(s) missing]

20 October 1875
Dear father I write these few lines
hopeing to find you better than it
leves us at present my mother as
been very ill and me my self
and I am a bit better Dear father
we think you have quite forgot us all
my sister Ann takes it hard at
you not writing oftener I must
tel you that sister Ann as to nice
boys the boldest is a fine little
fellow well I must tell you what
a stout young man my brother
Alfred as got and Thirza is a
stout young womman poor Ann
is very thin Ann usband and
Alfrted works at aldwarke

main pit Edward Uttley sends his
kindest love to you he has a large
famuley they have nine children
uncles and hants send their kindest
love to you we dont live far
from hant rebacco france I
often play with there little boy
my hant often say I am like
my father there oldest boy
William as been dead fifteen mounths
my uncle John as been over from
barring furnace and he looked
very well Dear father you would

Would hardly know Greasbrough
now if you seed it we have got
a new congregational church and I go
to that school

Dear father Mother would
like to no if they would alow
you our likeness Dear father
you never name me in you
letters but I can sit down and
write a letter to you now
Dear father my mother wants
to now if you ever hear of
been sat free we all send
kindest and dearest love to
you and God bless you
and 1,000 kisses for our Dear
father from your Dear
son William

Newcastle Hospital
January 26 1876
Sir
I have the honour to forward my
name to your notice for favourable con-
sideration having now completed 10 years
1 month & 13 days probation out of 12 years
6 months & 15 days – I have been a contractor
about 2 years and during the whole term
of my probation have had but 2 reports
of break of rules
I have been under Dr Mayhew now
for several months and I hope [to] say
that I have given him every satisfaction.
I can but ask that I may, like
others, have a trial on my ticket of leave,
and I feel assured you will
have no future cause to regret the leniency.
I am Sir
Yours respectfully
The Hon'ble
The Acting [Convict?] General
Perth

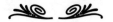

March 10th 1876

My Dear Sister
I rite to you once more hoping you and your husband and
children are in good health as it leaves me a present
thanks be to God for it and not to the dicetfullnes of
men on Earth – I am sorry that I have troubled all of you
much as I do think it is Either the trouble or the
expence but any way I do not think that I have given you
as mutch trouble as you have caused me and it is not the
riting and Expence that I have had to pussel mysefe with
that is given me all my trouble of mind no I have tryed
hard to hould a coraspondence with you all and I have
heard of you receiving my letters but no anseers and it
is that what Greaves me to my Hart yease I [wanted?] the
mother that whould answered them.

*Joshua Sykes My Dear Brother your mother I do believe
whas my mother and shee was a good mother and a Father
likewise to me God rest her soul I do think that if shee
ad abeen living and had heard Judge; shee say that if
anybody took Sykes case in hand he whould git is freedom
again that was wehen I was tryed the second time when he
said that I think ny poor m other would have tryed what
could be done for me and I think she is making
intersheshen for me now and have heard of some of the
prayers that as been ofered up been answered and I can
see a little of myself with one vilen thanks be to God I
never Enjoyed better Health myself with all the vileny.*

*dear brother I want you to rite to me will you and send
me your directions I wanted to see you in Rotherham
town Hall but thay whould not let me see you if I had
a seen you before I got tryed I should not have had any
Sentence at all and thay new that too: and mys sisters
nows what they said to them at Wakefield I wrote one
letter with 12 pages in it let me now if any of you got it
will you it contained a little information about a Hiway
robbery and murder and* JONATHAN WITTEKER I HAVE
NOTHING TO DO *I do not want the police nor detective
to* WITH IT ONLY I WAS TOULD ALL ABOUT IT *Get ould of
it as ther was a reward* BY ONE OF THE PARTY THE SAME
NIGHT IT HAPPENED *out at the time happened no more*
AND I ALWAY KEPT IT A SEACRET BUT THE VILLIND NO
MORE *I remain your afectanate Brother W.S.*

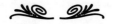

I SHOULD NOT HAVE DONE SO TO YOU

*John Dear Brother I heard you was over at Greasboro
and you was looking very well and it gave me grate
plesure to hear it as I have often wondered if you wher
living or dead I could not think of you whear alive
what you whould not rite to me I allways thought I
had a brother in you but no: and when I began ton
think about I culd call to mind that night when you
came to se me at Rotherham and wat you said and
then never to come to se me no more I should not have
done so to you no I should have come to se you John I
should have come to se you John I should never have
done as you have so no more at preasant from your
afectonate Brother W. S. still untill death part us
John I remain so*

Dear husban I ham grved
to my hart A bout my
Ann I have had her
Both times of her
confindments and
ly shee gating on
gain
We hall sends out
nearst and dearsted
Love to you
with A 1000 kiss
Dear Husband you
must excuse writing

14 May 1879 To Well Sinkers
in care of Mr C. Adams
William Sykes –
When I went to New-
castle I looked at
the Agreement and
I find you and your
mate were right in
what you said 5
shilling foot for every
five feet I did not
beleive that I made
that bargain with yous
but I see now that
I did W.T.
I am quite willing to settle
to settle with you when
I here from either of yous
yous plase send
word your James Ward

Greasbro' Vicarage
Rotherham
Novr. 28. 1890.
Sir,
A parishioner of mine has been to
see me relative to his father William Sykes
who, at the Christmas Assizes at Leeds in 1865
was sentenced to transportation [I believe] for
life. He is at present at Toodyay Newcastle,
Western Australia. He has 2 sons and 2
daughters and they would gladly pay his
fare home if the Government would permit
him to have his liberty. I believe that his
sentence was owing to his complicity in a
poaching affray which resulted in the
murder of a keeper. William Sykes at that
time resided in the neighbouring parish of
Masbro' but his wife and sons live in this
parish of Greasbro'.
I am, Sir
Your obedient Servant
(sd) J. Brock Beard.

The Rt. Hon.
G Mathews Esq. MP.

Whitehall
5th February 1891
Sir,
I have the honour to transmit
to you a copy of a letter from the
Rev'd J Beard, in which he petitions
that a convict named William Sykes
may be allowed to return to this Country.
The Depositions cannot be
obtained, but it appears from a
newspaper report and other documents
in the Home Office that Sykes was
Convicted of Manslaughter at the
York County Assizes on the 13th December
1865, was sentenced to Penal Servitude
for Life and was sent to Western
Australia by the ship 'Norwood' on
the 6th April 1867. Sykes was one
of a gang of poachers, and he and
another man took the most active
part in the affray in which a game-
keeper was beaten to death with
sticks; Mr Justice Shee, who presided
at the trial, remarking in passing
sentence, that few persons would have
disagreed with a verdict of 'Murder'.

Sykes is now 61 to 63 years of
age, and it is perhaps unlikely that
if allowed to return to this country
he would relapse into crime, but
I should be much obliged if you

*would favour me with a report as to
the conduct of Sykes since his transportation
to the Colony in April 1867, and with
any observations you might wish to
offer upon the application now under
consideration.*

*I have the honour to be
Your obedient Servant
E. [indecipherable]*

MINUTE PAPER NO. *551/91*
From the Home Secretary
Dated 5 2 1891
SUBJECT: *Release of Wm Sykes to return to England*
Letter from Rev'd J Beard

To
His Excellency
The Governor
I beg to forward for the information
of Your Excellency, the prison history
of the late William Sykes Reg No
9589. A minute received on the
12th inst. from the Resident magistrate
at Newcastle [indecipherable] the Superintend't of
Poor Relief conveys the information
that Sykes died in the hospital
at Newcastle on or about the 4th or 5th
of January last and that his effects
are but of trifling value.
[signature indecipherable]
Inspector of Prisons
14/3/91

ACKNOWLEDGMENTS

Alexandra Hasluck's book contains many of the primary source documents known to her at the time of her research and writing in the early to mid-1950s. Since then, significant additional documentation has come to light, including the surgeon's and religious instructor's records of the *Norwood's* voyage to the Swan River and the materials relating to the family's efforts to have the ageing William repatriated. Also previously unexamined or unknown were the details of the trial of Booth and Savage for night poaching and the existence of William Sykes's letters to his family. Genealogical research, assisted by Mr Howard Gibb, revealed the birth of a fifth child to Myra, providing some – though far from all – answers to a number of puzzling aspects of William's behaviour. The information on poaching and social and political protest in the period also adds a new dimension to the story of Myra and William Sykes. The present book is based on all known sources of information, the most important of which are included below and in the Appendix, 'These Few Lines: The Toodyay Letters and Related Documents'.

I would also like to acknowledge the contribution of the following individuals and institutions to the research, writing and publication of this book.

Angelo Loukakis
Australian Studies Centre, Curtin University
Battye Library of Western Australian History
British Library
Brotherton Library, University of Leeds
Dennis Taylor
Institute of Dialectology and Folklife Studies (former),
    University of Leeds
Helen Littleton and staff of ABC Books
Tony Lynch, for drawing the maps
Maureen Seal
National Centre for English Cultural Tradition,
    Sheffield University
National Maritime Museum (UK)
Professor J. D. A. Widdowson
Public Records Office of Western Australia
Gillian O'Mara
Rotherham Central Library, Local Records and
    Archives
Sheffield City Library
Sheffield University Library
State Library of Western Australia
Western Australian Folklore Archive, Curtin University
    of Technology
Sandra Goldbloom Zurbo, for fine editing

CHAPTER 1

1   *Sheffield Daily Telegraph*, 2 November 1865.

2   Evidence of keeper William Butler at Leeds assizes,
     Sheffield Daily Telegraph, 22 December 1865, and
     also mentioned by other witnesses and participants.
     There is also a brief, though often inaccurate,
     account of these events in Hopkins, H., *The Long
     Affray: The Poaching Wars 1760–1914*, Secker &
     Warburg, London, 1985, pp. 240–42.

3   See Peacock, A. J., *Bread or Blood*, London, 1965;
     Hobsbawm, E. & Rudé, G., *Captain Swing*,
     London, 1969; Thompson, E. P., *The Making of the
     English Working-Class*, Penguin, Harmondsworth
     (1963) 1968, *Whigs and Hunters: The Origins of
     the Black Act*, Penguin, Harmondsworth, 1975 and
     his *Customs in Common*, Penguin,
     Harmondsworth, 1991; see also Seal, G., 'Tradition
     and Protest in Nineteenth Century England and
     Wales', *Folklore*, 100:2, 1988.

4   Munsche, P. B., 'The Game Laws in Wiltshire,
     1750–1800' in J. S. Cockburn (ed), *Crime in
     England, 1550–1800*, London, 1977, p. 210. On
     this point see also Heath, R., *The English Peasant*,
     London, 1893, p. 33 and Zouch, H., *An Account*

of the Present Daring practices of Night-Hunters, and Poachers..., *etc.*, London, 1783, pp. 9ff for the same fears expressed in the 1780s, and p. 6 for an account of poachers vandalising the home of the Marquis of Rockingham.

5   Munsche, p. 210; see also Simon Schama's brief but evocative discussion of mediaeval forest poaching and outlawry in his *Landscape and Memory*, HarperCollins, London, 1995, pp. 142ff.

6   Munsche, p. 211.

7   Bovill, E. W., *English Country Life, 1780–1830*, London, 1962, pp. 177–8.

8   Bovill, p. 179.

9   Bovill, pp. 178–82.

10   The relationship between beliefs about common rights, enclosure, violent protest – a good deal of which had connections to poaching – and customary behaviour is a complex topic in itself. See, for example, Gifford, R., 'Guy Fawkes: Who Celebrated What? A Closer Look at 5th November in the Light of Captain Swing', in T. Buckland, & J. Wood (eds), *Aspects of British Calendar Customs*, Sheffield, 1993, who cites a Guy Fawkes night riot at the home of the Duke of Manchester in 1830. The Duke was a prime mover in the local anti-poaching organisation.

11   From Chitty, J., 'Observations on the Game Laws' (1816), quoted in D. Hay, 'Poaching and the Game Laws on Cannock Chase' in D. Hay et. al. (eds), *Albion's Fatal Tree: Crime and Society in Eighteenth Century England*, London, 1975, pp. 191, 194; see also Bovill, p. 179 for a similar statement from Sydney Smith.

12 Peacock, A. J., *Bread or Blood*, London, 1965, p. 38.

13 Bovill, pp. 179–80; also Heath, p. 134 and Thompson, F. M. L., *English Landed Society in the Nineteenth Century*, London, 1963, p. 142 for further evidence of the same attitudes among rural workers.

14 Rider Haggard, L. (ed.), *I Walked By Night* (1935), London, 1947, p. 186.

15 'Rufford Park Poacher', sung by Mr Joseph Taylor, Brigg, Lincs., 4 August 1906. Phonographed and noted by Percy Grainger; see *Journal of the Folk-Song Society*, London, vol. III, No. 12, May 1908, p. 187.

16 Sung by John Day, Hillingdon Union, Middlesex, 20 September 1913, noted by Cecil Sharp in *Journal of the Folk-Song Society*, vol. VIII, No. 31, 1931, p. 7; also a version collected from George 'Pop' Maynard, Copthorne, Sussex, by Ken Stubbs in 1954 and quoted in Lloyd, A. L., *Folksong in England*, London, 1969, p. 246.

17 Noted by Reverend John Broadwood before 1840 in L. E. Broadwood & J. A. Maitland, *English County Songs*, London, (1893) n.d., pp. 50–51; see also *Journal of the Folk-Song Society*, vol. 5, no. 19, 1915, p. 198 for a version collected in Herts., 1898 (1 verse only) and p. 199 for a Sussex version of 1907.

18 *Sheffield and Rotherham Advertiser*, 2 December 1865, p. 5.

19 In his study of social protesters transported to Australia, *Protest and Punishment: The Story of the Social and Political Protesters Transported to*

Australia, 1788–1868, Oxford University Press, Melbourne, 1978, George Rudé notes, not quite accurately, that William Sykes was 'The last poacher of all to land in Australia' (p. 154). In fact, Sykes was but one of a number of poachers transported aboard the *Norwood*, including his companions from the Silver Wood affray. However, as Rudé also points out, Sykes was not a social or political protester.

20   Poaching was also carried out in an organised manner as an illegal supply to metropolitan restaurants; it is possible that William Sykes and his friends took a small part in this lucrative black economy. See the letter of William Sykes to his brother Joshua, which suggests Sykes may have had some tentative connections with the world of serious crime. He had certainly known the shady Woodhouse for five years before the Silver Wood affray; see *Sheffield Daily Telegraph*, 22 December 1865.

CHAPTER 2

1   *Sheffield and Rotherham Independent* , 12 October 1865.

2   *Sheffield Daily Telegraph*, 13 October 1865.

3   *Sheffield and Rotherham Advertiser*, 14 October 1865.

4   *Sheffield Daily Telegraph*, 26 October 1865.

5   *Sheffield Daily Telegraph*, 2 November 1865.

6   *Sheffield Daily Telegraph*, 22 December 1865.

7   *Sheffield Daily Telegraph*, 18 October 1865.

8   *Rotherham and Masbrough Advertiser*, 28 October 1865.

9   *Sheffield Daily Telegraph*, 28 October 1865.

10   None of which harmed Jubb's professional
      standing. The following year he was appointed a
      tax and rates commissioner for the West Riding of
      Yorkshire, Statutes Public General 29° and 30°
      Victoriae, c. 58, 59 CAP. LIX.
11   *Sheffield Daily Telegraph*, 2 November 1865.
12   *Sheffield Daily Telegraph*, 4 November 1865.
13   *Sheffield Daily Telegraph*, 6 November 1865.
14   *Sheffield Daily Telegraph*, 8 November 1865.
15   *Rotherham and Masbrough Advertiser*, Nov 11,
      1865, p. 3.
16   *Sheffield Daily Telegraph*, Nov 8, 1865.
17   *Sheffield Daily Telegraph*, Nov 16, 1865.
18   *Sheffield Daily Telegraph*, 17 November 1865; see
      also *The Sheffield and Masbrough Advertiser*, 18
      November 1865.

CHAPTER 3

1   Myra is a name invented by the seventeenth-century
      poet Fulke Greville. It may be an anagram of
      'Mary' or come from the simplified Latin 'myrrh',
      familiar to Christians as one of the gifts brought by
      the Three Wise Men to the Christ-child. Myra was
      not unknown, but was far from a common female
      name at this time and in this place.
2   William's brother, Joshua, seems to have had a
      connection with the progressive side of politics.
3   *Parliamentary Papers*, 1842, vol. XVl, pp. 252–3.
4   *Baines's Yorkshire: History, Directory and
      Gazetteer of the County of York*, 2 vols, 1822 and
      1823, reprinted David & Charles, Newton Abbot,
      Devon, 1969, pp. 630–1; see also *Langdale's
      Topographical Dictionary of Yorkshire*, 1822.

5   *Langdale's Topographical Dictionary of Yorkshire*, 1822.

6   *Langdale's Topographical Dictionary of Yorkshire*, 1822.

7   *Baines's*, p. 257; see also Guest, J., *Relics and Records of Men and Manufacturers at or in the Neighbourhood of Rotherham* ..., paper read on 27 March 1865 before the Members of the Rotherham Literary and Scientific Society, reprinted by Rotherham Metropolitan Borough Council, 1980, pp. 43, 72, 83, 84, 88, 89, 93, 100.

8   Symons, J. C., in *Parliamentary Papers*, 1843, vol. XIV, E11, 93.

9   These are the dates in the census returns for 1871, 1881 and 1891. They do not tally with those given by Alexandra Hasluck in *Unwilling Emigrants*, p. 2.

10 *Murray's Hand-Book of Yorkshire*, p. 482.

11 Young, A., *General Report on Enclosures* (1808), London, 1971, 56–7.

12 Holt, J., *General View of the Agriculture of the County of Lancaster*, London, 1795, p. (i), and printed in all subsequent editions.

13 Quoted in Peacock, A. J, *Bread or Blood*, London, 1965, p. 20.

14 Thompson, E. P., *Customs in Common*, Penguin, Harmondsworth, 1991, p. 111.

15 Thompson, E. P., *Whigs and Hunters: The Origin of the Black Act*, Penguin, Harmondsworth, 1975; see also Zouch, H., *An Account of the Present Daring Practices of Night-Hunters and Poachers... etc.*, London, 1783.

16 Reaney, B., *The Class Struggle in Nineteenth Century Oxfordshire: The Social and Communal

Background to the Otmoor Disturbances of 1830 to 1835, Oxford, 1970, pp. 33–5.

17 Bean, J., *Crime in Sheffield from Deer Poaching to Gangsters, 1300 to the 1980s*, Sheffield City Libraries, 1987, pp. 29–37.

18 Gummer, G., *Reminiscences of Rotherham*, Rotherham, 1927, p. 116.

19 'Carolus Paulus', *Some Forgotten Facts in the History of Sheffield and Districts*, Sheffield, 1907.

20 *Sheffield Daily Telegraph*, 16 November 1865.

CHAPTER 4

1 They had also poached there at least once before, according to evidence at the trial; *Sheffield Daily Telegraph*, 15 November 1865.

2 *Sheffield Daily Telegraph*, 22 December 1865.

3 *Sheffield Daily Telegraph*.

4 *Sheffield Daily Telegraph*.

5 Mayhall, J., *The Annals and History of Leeds and Other Places in the County of York*, Leeds, 1860, p. 682.

6 *Sheffield and Rotherham Independent*, 26 December 1865 and *Sheffield Daily Telegraph*, 26 December 1865.

CHAPTER 5

1 *Sheffield Daily Telegraph*, 10 January 1866.

2 *Sheffield Daily Telegraph*, 11 January 1866.

3 *Sheffield Daily Telegraph*, 12 January 1866.

4 *Sheffield Daily Telegraph*, 10 January 1866.

5 *Sheffield Local Register*, 1865, 1866.

6 *The Sheffield Outrages: Report Presented to the Trade Unions Commissioners in 1867*.

7 Bean, J., op. cit., pp. 12ff.

8   *Sheffield Daily Telegraph*, 4 May 1867.
9   *Sheffield Daily Telegraph*, 23 October 1865, July
     1865, 7 July 1865 (3 incidents), 21 December
     1865.
10   *Sheffield Daily Telegraph*, 18 December 1868, then
     18 January (2 incidents), 29 January 29
     (3 incidents), 3 March (3 cases), 19 March, 7 April,
     9 April, 28 April, 31 May (2 cases), 30 June,
     10 July, 14 July, 25 July, 31 July, 18 August,
     8 September, 22 September (2 incidents) and
     6 October, 1868; see also Bean, pp. 40–2 and
     Hopkins, H., *The Long Affray*, *passim*.

CHAPTER 6
1   Hasluck, op. cit., p. 17.
2   *Sheffield Local Register*, 1865 and 1866.
3   *Cornhill Magazine*, vol. XIII, January–June 1866,
     p. 497 and Hasluck, op. cit., pp. 17–18.
4   Hughes, R., *The Fatal Shore: A History of the
     Transportation of Convicts to Australia,
     1787–1868*, London, 1987.
5   The colony officially elected to become a penal
     settlement in 1849.
6   We read no more of Woodhouse in Myra's
     subsequent correspondence. Given the depth of
     local antagonism towards the man, he may well
     have moved elsewhere.
7   There is a possibility that such a petition was made,
     though a search of CO 397/28 (part 2),
     Correspondence 1856–73 and associated papers
     revealed no evidence.

Chapter 7

1 Saunders, Dr, 'The Surgeon's Day Log: Convict Ship "Norwood", 1867', Battye Library Q910.45 SAU, transcribed by John Kelly.

2 This was one of the letters missing from the Sykes Papers.

3 'Norwoodiana or Sayings and Doings on Route to Western Australia: A Manuscript Journal Made During the 1867 Voyage of the Convict Ship Norwood, April to July 1867 by William Irwin (Religious Instructor)', (transcribed by B. & T. Dent, 1996, from original ms. in Mitchell Library, Sydney), copy Battye Library.

4 Norwoodiana 8, p. 5. For a more accurate and knowledgeable account of the language of the Aborigines in Perth and surrounding regions, see Lyon, R. M., 'A Glance at the Manners and Language of the Aboriginal Inhabitants of Western Australia: With a Short Vocabulary', *Perth Gazette and Western Australian Journal*, March–April 1833, quoted in N. Green (ed.), *Nyungar – The People: Aboriginal Customs in the Southwest of Australia*, Perth, 1979, pp. 148–180, and *passim*.

Chapter 8

1 There were 30 pensioner guards with 17 wives, 14 sons, 16 daughters and another four cabin passengers or, possibly, soldiers.

2 Haswell, G., *Ten Shanties Sung on the Australian Run*, 1879, Antipodes Press, 1992.

3 Thought to be another name for the Cape Pigeon.

4 Arriving at Adelaide (SA) in 1840, Ellen Moger wrote home to her parents: 'Poor little Alfred was

the first that died on the 30th of Oct, and on the 8th of Nov, dear Fanny went and three days after, on the 11th, the dead babe was taken from me.' Things had improved a little in the quarter century following, though illness and childbirth were still very dangerous aboard ship; see Haynes, R., *Life and Death in the Age of Sail: The Passage to Australia*, UNSW Press, Sydney, 2003.

5   *Cornhill Magazine*, April 1866.

6   Bateson, C., *The Convict Ships, 1787–1868*, Reed, Sydney, 1974, p. 377.

7   *Cornhill Magazine*, op. cit.

8   Rudé, G., op. cit., p. 154, n. 39.

9   Convict Department of Western Australia Convict Shipping and Description List No. 30 'Norwood', Battye Library.

CHAPTER 9

1   It has also been asserted that the Chinese were in contact with mainland Australia in the 1430s and even, if more difficult to ascertain, some centuries earlier. Certainly there was contact through Macassan fishermen, probably with Portuguese traders in the fifteenth century; see Appleyard, R. & Manford, T., *The Beginning: European Discovery and Early Settlement of Swan River Western Australia*, University of Western Australia Press, Perth, 1979, ch. 1.

2   Dampier wrote this in a popular account of his voyage. His official report is much more accurate and contains no such prejudiced statements calculated to appeal to the baser Eurocentric stereotypes.

3   Fitch, V., *Eager for Labour: The Swan River Indenture*, Hesperian Press, Perth, 2003.

4   Quoted in Green, 'Aborigines and White Settlers in the Nineteenth Century', in Stannage, C. T. (ed), *A New History of Western Australia,* University of Western Australia Press, Nedlands, 1981, p. 89.

5   Published in *The Looking Glass*, London, 1830.

6   See, for instance, Appleyard & Manford, pp. 148–63.

7   Though it has also been argued that the colony lacked capital rather than labour and that the convicts would increase the market for local consumption. *Fremantle Prison Newsletter*, no. 11, June 1999.

8   There had been transportation to Western Australia before this. Boys from the Parkhurst Prison on the Isle of Wight were sent to the colony between 1842 and 1849. *Fremantle Prison Newsletter*, no. 13, December 1999.

9   Smith, E. Langley, *Convict Prison Fremantle*, E. Langley Smith, Perth, 1997, pp. 27–8.

10   Stannage, C., *The People of Perth*, Perth, 1979, p. 94. Only male convicts were transported to the Swan River.

11   Erickson, R., *Dictionary of West Australians 1829–1914*, University of Western Australia Press, Nedlands, vol. 4, pt. 1, p. 135.

12   Hasluck, A., *Unwilling Emigrants*, Oxford University Press, Melbourne, 1959, p. 80.

13   According to Erickson, R. & O'Mara, G. *Dictionary Of Western Australians 1829–1914*, University of Western Australia Press, Nedlands, 1994, Teale received this documentation of

completion of sentence in 1898. If accurate, this means he must have been convicted of further crimes as his original 20 year sentence would have expired in 1886, possibly earlier.

14　*Sheffield & Rotherham Independent*, 12, 13, 14, 21, 28 December 1867.

15　*Sheffield & Rotherham Advertiser*, 21 March 1868, p. 5.

16　*Sheffield Daily Telegraph*, 4 February 1868.

17　As for Sykes and company, Mr Campbell Foster was counsel.

18　*Sheffield Daily Telegraph*, 10 February 1868.

19　Platts had turned up at the trial so drunk he was, conveniently perhaps, unable to testify, *Sheffield Daily Telegraph*, 10 February 1868.

20　*Sheffield and Rotherham Independent*, 28 December 1867. The correspondent gave the name Henry Moore, of Doncaster.

21　*Sheffield Daily Telegraph*, 30 March 1868.

CHAPTER 10

1　Evans, A., *Fanatic Heart: A Life of John Boyle O'Reilly 1844–1890*, University of Western Australia Press, Nedlands, 1997, p. 98; see also Sullivan, C. W. III, *Fenian Diary: Denis B Cashman Aboard the Hougoumont, 1867–1868*, Wolfhound Press, Dublin, 2001.

2　Hasluck, A., op. cit., p. 75.

3　O'Reilly, J., *Moondyne*, published in Boston in 1879, in Australia the following year and frequently reprinted since.

4　The case of the transported Irish rebels excited considerable interest at the time. 'Correspondence

Entry Books of Letters from Secretary of State. Despatches 1856–73', CO 397/28 (part 2); see also Evans, op. cit.

5   'Correspondence Entry Books of Letters from Secretary of State. Despatches 1856 – 73', CO 397/28 (part 2).

6   The last being as late as 1989, just two years before the prison was decommissioned. Bosworth, M., *Convict Fremantle*, University of Western Australia Press, Nedlands, 2004, p. 80.

7   Elliot, I, *Moondyne Joe: The Man and the Myth*, University of Western Australia Press, Nedlands, 1979 and Seal, G., *The Outlaw Legend: A Cultural Tradition in Britain, America and Australia*, Cambridge University Press, Melbourne, 1996, p. 144.

8   From O'Reilly's recently discovered Western Australian verse manuscript, quoted in full in Evans, p. 125.

CHAPTER 11

1   Not 1872, as Alexandra Hasluck surmised. From the internal evidence of Myra's birthday falling on a Tuesday, 17 March, as it did in 1874, and the election of Anthony John Mundella as MP for Sheffield in the 1874 general election, the letter could not have been written in 1872.

2   There is a black-edged letter from Joshua Sykes to the Hargreaves family expressing sorrow at the death of young William. It is dated August 30, 1874 and proffers Joshua's reasons for not being able to attend the funeral. It suggests that Joshua was doing quite well for himself and his family,

with a business, assistants and plans to spend 11 or 12 days at the seaside. Copy in Rotherham Library Local Studies holdings 'Who's Who' file for Sykes.

3 An empty envelope dated 19 January 1876 and postmarked 'Rotherham' is part of the Sykes Papers; see Hasluck, A., *Unwilling Emigrants*, p. 84.

CHAPTER 12

1 Erickson, R., *Old Toodyay and Newcastle*, Toodyay Shire Council, 1974, pp. 214–5, 283–4, 318, 330, 351.

2 The letter is at 564A in the Battye Library.

3 Hasluck, op. cit., p. 102, citing a now-lost document found with the letters in the kangaroo-skin pouch.

4 See Appendix, *These Few Lines*.

5 Ward, his wife and his partner established the first homestead in this area. There would have been an ongoing demand for water as the area developed. Erickson, R., op. cit., p. 183.

6 William does not appear in the Western Australian General Railways lists of employees for the period and so was probably not a permanent employee.

7 Stannage, op. cit., p. 193.

8 Holyday, C., *Into the West: When Australia's bush poet Henry Lawson came to Western Australia*, Hesperian Press, Perth, 2005.

9 There is some uncertainty about the exact date of death, some documents claiming William Sykes died at Newcastle (Toodyay) Hospital on 5 January, while the Toodyay cemetery register has him being buried on 4 January; see note 10.

10   This information comes from Hasluck, p. 155, note 65. According to Young, J. (comp.), 'Toodyay Cemeteries 1857–1940', Battye Library Typescript PR2640, 1983, p.17, a W. Sykes, aged 63 years, TOL 9589, was buried in the Anglican section of the cemetery on 4 January 1891. There is some controversy about the exact location of the grave.

11   This letter incorrectly states that Sykes was tried at York. Possibly as a consequence of this mistake the bureaucrats had been unable to locate the trial depositions. Despite lack of access to these they obviously had fairly detailed information about the trial from another source.

CHAPTER 13

1   *Rotherham & Masbro' Advertiser*, 4 May 1895, p. 6.

2   Fletcher, J. S., *A Picturesque History of York*.

3   Fletcher.

4   The quality of the water supply was an ongoing problem, especially in and around Sheffield. *A Short History of Sheffield*, Sheffield Libraries and Information Services, 1995, n.p., p. 4. The issue often featured in local papers.

5   Reports of the campaign appeared in the *Sheffield Daily Telegraph* from July to November 1868, and, rather less floridly, in the *Sheffield and Rotherham Independent*.

6   Myra's always shaky spelling seems to have had the better of her that year, or perhaps someone else filled in the census form. The name was often spelt this way by the newspapers.

7   Entry of Birth No. 224 in registration District of
        Rotherham, subdistrict of Kimberworth, York.

8   It is just possible that Frederick was not Myra's
        child, but that of the then 14-year-old Ann.
        Mothers would sometimes claim such illegitimate
        births as their own in order to protect the daughter
        from possible censure. But there is no evidence of
        Ann being pregnant and the only extant
        documentation names Myra as mother.

9   The 1891 census, Class RG12, Piece 3853, Folio 98
        also records the presence of a Thomas Wilcock, 21,
        and another coal miner.

10   *Rotherham & Masbro' Advertiser*, 22 December
        1894.

11   Taylor, D., William Sykes website at
        <website.lineone.net/~bill.sykes>.

12   *West Australian*, 6 June 2000.

Appleyard, R. & Manford, T. 1979, *The Beginning: European Discovery and Early Settlement of Swan River Western Australia*, University of Western Australia Press, Perth.

Archer, J. 1990, *By a Flash and a Scare: Incendiarism, Animal Maiming and Poaching in East Anglia, 1815–1870*, Oxford University Press, Oxford.

Baines, E. 1822 and 1823, *Baines's Yorkshire: History, Directory and Gazetteer of the County of York*, 2 vols (reprinted 1969, David & Charles, Newton Abbot, Devon).

Bateson, C. 1974, *The Convict Ships, 1787–1868*, Reed, Sydney (first published 1959).

Bean, J. 1987, *Crime in Sheffield from Deer Poachers to Gangsters, 1300 to the 1980s*, Sheffield City Libraries, Sheffield.

Bosworth, M. 2004, *Convict Fremantle: A Place of Promise and Punishment*, University of Western Australia Press, Perth.

Bovill, E. W. 1962, *English Country Life*, 1780–1830, London.

Broadwood, L. E. & Maitland, J. A. n.d. (1893), *English County Songs*, Cramer & Co., London.

'Carolus Paulus' 1907, *Some Forgotten Facts in the History of Sheffield and Districts*, Sheffield.

Carter, M. 1980, *Peasants and Poachers: A Study of Rural Disorder in Norfolk*, Boydell Press, Woodbridge.

Chitty, J. 1975, 'Observations on the Game Laws' (1816), in D. Hay et al. (eds), *Albion's Fatal Tree: Crime and Society in Eighteenth Century England*, Allen & Unwin, London.

Commercial Directory of Sheffield, *Rotherham and the Neighbourhood 1825–1896*.

Convict Department of Western Australia Convict Shipping and Description List No. 30, 'Norwood', Battye Library.

Erickson, R. 1979, *Dictionary of West Australians 1829–1914*, University of Western Australia Press, Nedlands.

—— & O'Mara, G. 1994, *Dictionary Of Western Australians 1829–1914*, University of Western Australia Press, Nedlands.

Erickson, R. 1974, *Old Toodyay and Newcastle*, Toodyay Shire Council, Toodyay.

Evans, A. 1997, *Fanatic Heart: A Life of John Boyle O'Reilly 1844–1890*, University of Western Australia Press, Nedlands.

Evans, H. Tobit 1910, *Rebecca and Her Daughters*, Thomas Richards, Cardiff.

Fitch, V. 2003, *Eager for Labour: The Swan River Indenture*, Hesperian Press, Perth.

Fletcher, J. S. 1899–1901, *A Picturesque History of Yorkshire*, 3 vols, London.

Fremantle Prison Newsletter, 1999–2000, Fremantle Prison, Fremantle.

Gifford, R. 1993, 'Guy Fawkes: Who Celebrated What? A Closer Look at 5th November in the Light of Captain Swing', in T. Buckland & J. Wood (eds), *Aspects of British Calendar Customs*, Sheffield Academic Press, Sheffield.

Green, N. 1984, *Broken Spears: Aboriginals and Europeans in the Southwest of Australia*, Focus Education Services, Perth.

—— (ed.) 1979, *Nyungar – The People: Aboriginal Customs in the Southwest of Australia*, Creative Research Publishers and Mt Lawley College, Perth.

—— 1981 'Aborigines and White Settlers in the Nineteenth Century', in C. T. Stannage (ed.), *A New History of Western Australia*, University of Western Australia Press, Nedlands.

Guest, J. 1865, 'Relics and Records of Men and Manufacturers at or in the Neighbourhood of Rotherham ...', paper read on the 27th of March, before the Members of the Rotherham Literary and Scientific Society, reprinted 1980, Rotherham Metropolitan Borough Council.

Gummer, G. 1927, *Reminiscences of Rotherham*, H. Garnett, Rotherham.

Haggard, Rider L. (ed.) 1947, *I Walked By Night* (1935), Nicholson & Watson, London.

Hasluck, A. 1959, *Unwilling Emigrants*, Oxford University Press, Melbourne.

Haswell, G. (coll.) 1992, *Ten Shanties Sung on the Australian Run* (first published 1879), The Antipodes Press, Perth.

Haynes, R. 2003, *Life and Death in the Age of Sail: The Passage to Australia*, UNSW Press, Sydney.

Heath, R. 1893, *The English Peasant*, Methuen, London.

Hey, D. 1979, *The Making of South Yorkshire*, Moorland Publishing, South Yorkshire.

Hobsbawm, E. & Rudé, G. 1969, *Captain Swing*, Pimlico, London.

Holt, J. 1795, *General View of the Agriculture of the County of Lancaster*, Allen Lane, London.

Holyday, C. 2005, *Into the West: When Australia's bush poet Henry Lawson came to Western Australia*, Hesperian Press, Victoria Park.

Hopkins, H. 1985, *The Long Affray: The Poaching Wars 1760–1914*, Secker & Warburg, London.

Jones, D. 1973, *Before Rebecca: Popular Protest in Wales, 1793–1835*, London.

—— 1989, *Rebecca's Children: A Study of Rural Society, Crime and Protest*, Clarendon Press, Oxford.

Karpeles, M. (ed.) 1974, *Cecil Sharp's Collection of English Folk Songs*, vol. 2, Oxford University Press, Oxford.

Kelly's Directory of Sheffield and Rotherham and Neighbourhood, Kelly & Co., from 1848.

Langdale's Topographical Dictionary of Yorkshire, 1822.

'List of Monumental Inscriptions in Greasborough [sic] Churchyard prior to the Creation of a Garden of Remembrance in or about 1965', 1967, typescript, Sheffield Library.

Lloyd, A. L. 1967, *Folksong in England*, Lawrence & Wishart, London.

Machin, F. n.d. (1958?), *The Yorkshire Miners: A History*, 2 vols, National Union of Mineworkers, Yorkshire Area, Barnsley.

Manning, R. 1993, *Hunters and Poachers: A Cultural and Social History of Unlawful Hunting in England, 1485–1640*, Clarendon Press, Oxford.

Mayhall, J. 1860 (other years bound in), *The Annals and History of Leeds and Other Places in the County of York*, Leeds.

Morsley, C. (ed.) 1979, *News from the English Countryside, 1750–1850*, Harrap, London.

Munsche, P. B. 1977, 'The Game Laws in Wiltshire, 1750–1800', in J. S. Cockburn (ed.), *Crime in England, 1550–1800*, Methuen, London.

Murray's Hand-Book of Yorkshire 1867, London.

Irwin, W. 1867, '"Norwoodiana", or Sayings and Doings on Route to Western Australia: A Manuscript Journal Made During the 1867 Voyage of the Convict Ship Norwood, April to July 1867 by William Irwin (Religious Instructor)', B. & T. Dent, transcribers, 1996, from original ms., Mitchell Library, Sydney), copy Battye Library, Perth.

Parish Register of St Mary's, Greasbrough, transcript, Rotherham Library Local Studies.

Parliamentary Papers 1842, vol. XVl.

Peacock, A. J. 1965, *Bread or Blood*, Gollancz, London.

Pollard, S. (ed.) 1971, *The Sheffield Outrages: Report Presented to the Trade Unions Commissioners in 1867*, Adams & Dart, Bath.

Reaney, B. 1970, *The Class Struggle in Nineteenth Century Oxfordshire: The Social and Communal Background to the Otmoor Disturbances of 1830 to 1835*, History Workshop, Oxford.

Rotherham and Masbrough Advertiser.

Rudé, G. 1978, *Protest and Punishment: The Story of the Social and Political Protesters Transported to Australia, 1788–1868*, Oxford University Press, Melbourne.

Saunders, Dr 1867, *The Surgeon's Day Log: Convict Ship 'Norwood'*, John Kelly, transcriber, Battye Library Q910.45 SAU.

Schama, S. 1995, *Landscape and Memory*, HarperColllins, London.

Seal, G. 1988, 'A Kangaroo-skin Pouch of Letters', *History Today*, 38:1, January.

——, 'Dear Husband', ABC Radio, first broadcast 1987.

—— 1988, 'Tradition and Protest in Nineteenth Century England and Wales', *Folklore*, 100:2.

Sheffield Daily Telegraph.

Sheffield Local Register, 1855–70, published by *The Independent*.

Sheffield and Rotherham Independent.

Sheffield Miscellany, 1897, Sheffield.

Smith, E. L. 1997, *Convict Prison Fremantle*, E. Langley Smith, Perth.

Stannage, C. T. 1979, *The People of Perth: A Social History of Western Australia's Capital City*, Perth City Council, Perth.

—— (ed.) 1981, *A New History of Western Australia*, University of Western Australia Press, Nedlands.

——, Saunders, K. & Nile, R. (eds) 1998, *Paul Hasluck in Australian History*, University of Queensland Press, St Lucia.

Sullivan, C. W. III 2001, *Fenian Diary: Denis B Cashman Aboard the Hougoumont, 1867–1868*, Wolfhound Press, Dublin.

Sykes file, Local Studies Section, Rotherham Library, Yorkshire.

Taylor, D., William Sykes website at <www.website.lineone.net/~bill.sykes>.

Taylor, J. (ed.) 1879 (1st edn, 1862), *The Illustrated Guide to Sheffield and the Surrounding Districts*, Sheffield.

Thompson, E. P. 1968, *The Making of the English Working-Class*, Penguin, Harmondsworth.

—— 1975, *Whigs and Hunters: The Origins of the Black Act*, Penguin, Harmondsworth.

—— 1991, *Customs in Common*, Penguin, Harmondsworth.

Thompson, F. M. L. 1963, *English Landed Society in the Nineteenth Century*, Routledge and Paul, London.

Turton, K. 2001, *At Her Majesty's Pleasure: The Killing of William Lilley – Gamekeeper*, Rotherwood Press, Rotherham.

Tweedale, G. 1995, *Steel City: Entrepreneurship, Strategy and Technology in Sheffield 1743–1993*, Oxford University Press, Oxford.

United Kingdom Census, 1871, 1881, 1891.

Vickers, J. 1978, *A Popular History of Sheffield*, EP Publishing, Sheffield.

Williams, D. 1955, *The Rebecca Riots: A Study in Agrarian Discontent*, Cardiff.

William Sykes Papers, Battye Library of Western Australian History, Perth.

Wilson, C. 1994, 'Greasbrough: A History', typescript, Blackburn School.

Young, A. 1971, *General Report on Enclosures (1808)*, London.

Young, J. (comp.) 1983, 'Toodyay Cemeteries 1857–1940', Battye Library Typescript PR2640.

Zouch, H. 1783, *An Account of the Present Daring Practices of Night-Hunters, and Poachers ... etc.*, London.